The work of many prominent social scientists—in writing,
research, analysis and synthesis—is of interest and
importance far beyond the boundaries of traditional
disciplines and sub-fields. It is to present such
works—diverse in subject and audience—that the
SAGE LIBRARY OF SOCIAL RESEARCH
exists. Volumes in this series are published
originally in paper; clothbound library editions
are also available.

SAGE PUBLICATIONS
The Publishers of Professional Social Science
Beverly Hills ● London

the same, and all *living* trusts aren't the same. The wrong trust can cause problems, while the right trust can solve problems. A trust which is right for one person's circumstances may be the wrong trust for another person's circumstances.

You won't find any blank forms in this book. As you read further you will understand that there simply are not enough pages available (without producing an encyclopedia) to include forms for all of the possible choices you should make. Most forms are too simplified, and too "boiler-plate" in nature, to enable you to adopt a living trust which will fully meet your needs.

When you're finished with this book, you will be able to decide whether a trust would be helpful to you, and you will be able to select the *right* trust for your needs. If you decide to purchase forms to establish your own living trust, you will be more prepared to select the *right* forms, instead of using forms which may not be appropriate for your needs. If you decide to employ a professional to prepare your living trust, or assist you in its preparation, you will be in a better position to ask the right questions, and obtain maximum benefits from the services of that professional.

Sadly, there are a lot of living trust "experts" these days, who talk to people about forming living trusts and want to sell them products or services, who may be more concerned with getting your money than in truly assuring your financial security and fully attaining your estate planning objectives. Happily, there are also those who know what they're talking about and can be of real assistance to you. After you have finished this book, you will be able to spot the "phony" so-called expert a mile away.

Dwight F. Bickel
Boise, Idaho

# IS PROBATE ALL THAT BAD?

*QUICK PREVIEW*

> **IT IS FAIR TO REACH THE FOLLOWING CONCLUSIONS ABOUT PROBATE:**
>
> (1) **IT'S NOT A PLEASANT EXPERIENCE FOR MOST FAMILIES. IT IS COSTLY AND TIME CONSUMING, AND YOU LOSE MUCH OF YOUR PRIVACY.**
>
> (2) **MOST PEOPLE WON'T GAIN ANY BENEFITS FROM PROBATE.**
>
> (3) **HOWEVER, LIKE A BAD-TASTING MEDICINE, IF YOU HAVE A PROBLEM WHICH PROBATE CAN CURE, YOU'D BETTER TAKE THE MEDICINE — BUT YOU DON'T HAVE TO TAKE THE WHOLE BOTTLE OF MEDICINE! PROBATE ONLY ENOUGH ASSETS TO GET THE BENEFITS YOU NEED.**

Just about everyone now knows that a person can avoid probate by using a living trust. We'll discuss how that is done later in this book, but let's first think about whether probate is so bad that you ought to try to avoid it, and whether everyone should try to avoid it.

When the owner of anything of value dies, a legal question is presented: Who is the new owner of that property? Sometimes that question is automatically answered by provisions of the property laws or other areas of the law, and in this book we will refer to those cases as "non-probate transfers" of ownership. In order for there to be a non-probate transfer of ownership of your assets, you must make certain arrangements or take certain actions during your lifetime. In all likelihood, if you have not prearranged for a non-probate transfer of all of your assets, your estate will have to be probated.

If you are single, and do not make some special arrangements for avoiding probate, your estate will have to pass through probate when you die. If you are married, you may be able to avoid probate when the first spouse dies (state laws often readily permit non-probate transfers between husband and wife), but if you haven't arranged for a non-probate transfer, the estate will have to pass through probate proceedings when the second spouse dies, or if both spouses should die in a common disaster.

A probate proceeding is a court proceeding, in which a judge decides the legal questions concerning who will be the new owner of the deceased person's property, and supervises the settlement of the deceased person's affairs and the distribution of his or her estate. This sounds simple, but simplicity is just about the last term people who have gone through the probate of a relative's estate would use to describe what they experienced.

Probate proceedings are not exactly the same in every state, but there are many similarities. Most states have a simple and inexpensive procedure for administering *small estates*, usually $25,000 or less in total asset value. Most states have a procedure for an *informal* or *nonintervention* probate proceeding if there are no disputes among the family members and certain other conditions are met. Sometimes there are abbreviated, or *summary* proceedings when one spouse dies and all of the property is to pass to the surviving spouse. If you don't meet your state's specific rules for one of these time and cost savers, your estate will have to go through the full complicated probate process.

To make life even more miserable for the deceased person's family, states do not fully recognize each other's probate proceedings. There will have to be a separate court proceeding in every state in which the deceased person owned real estate which must pass through probate. And, you will probably find that the lawyer who handles one of the proceedings isn't licensed to practice law in the other state, so it will be necessary to hire another lawyer in that state.

There are three very real problems with probate, and those problems exist to a greater or lesser degree in all states, and with every estate: *cost; lack of privacy*, and *delays.*

## The First Problem — Cost of Probate

Even when informal or nonintervention probate is available, the family will probably have to hire an attorney in each state where a probate is required. "Do-it-yourself" probate is possible, but the likelihood of problems is so great that it is not advisable, and many who try it end up hiring an attorney before the proceedings are completed. Some states have laws which specify the fees which probate attorneys may charge, and other states leave the fee to be negotiated between the client and the attorney.

The attorney fees will usually range from around $500 for very small and simple estates to percentage fees of seven per cent or more of the total value of the estate. It has been my observation that even when attorney fees are supposed to be based upon time charges, the value of the estate usually gets taken into consideration. A person should ask questions locally in order to determine customary probate attorney fee costs in a particular area. Be certain that you ask some people who have *paid* probate attorney fees, as attorneys have a way of underestimating what it should cost to probate estates until you ask them to actually take care of a specific probate.

There are usually numerous additional probate costs for court filing fees, publication of notices in newspapers, personal representative fees, appraisal fees, and other expenses.

When the bills are all added up, you will probably find that somewhere between 3% and 12% of the value of the estate will have been spent for probate costs. Even at the lower end of that scale, these costs represent a significant portion of the deceased person's lifetime of work, investment, and savings.

## The Second Problem — Lack of Privacy

Probate court files are almost always public records. That means anyone can look through the contents of a probate file. If you've always wondered about what someone you know is worth, or what that family is going to do about a certain "black sheep" child or relative, just wait until a few months after that person's death and go down to the probate court and read the probate file. You'll see it all!

With only a few exceptions, a complete inventory of all property, investments, and other assets is required to be filed with the court. The will is always required to be placed in the probate file. If your estate passes through probate, nosy people can find out if you had a child you hadn't publicly admitted, whether you disinherited one of your children or other relatives, whether you left anything to your church, and just about everything else about what you had and who will get it.

## The Third Problem — Delays

Delays abound in probate. Some lawyers just

don't get in any hurry to take care of probate cases, because the court doesn't impose many deadlines and generally doesn't enforce whatever deadlines there are, as long as no one makes a fuss. Whenever court hearings are required, there are usually scheduling delays to find a date when both your attorney and the court's calendar match up. Most states require a several-month delay in the distribution of assets following publication of a *Notice to Creditors* of the deceased person. If the will is contested, or the family is fighting, there will be more court hearings and delays. If informal or nonintervention proceedings were not available, there may have to be repeated hearings for approval of proposed sales of various properties and assets owned by the deceased person.

In most states, it's just about impossible to complete a probate proceeding in less than six months after a person's death. Nine or twelve months are more customary. And the clerks at the probate court don't even raise an eyebrow in surprise if a probate case is still open a year and a half or more after a person's death.

And while the probate drags on, the heirs wait, the fees continue to mount up, and the condition of the property often worsens and its value declines, for lack of an owner and that owner's personal attention.

## There Are a Few Situations
## Where Probate Helps

In fairness to probate lawyers, it should be said that there are a few situations (very few) when probate is, in fact, desirable in spite of these problems. For example, probate lawyers all get very excited about the benefits of probate in "cutting off" creditor claims. Generally, state law provides that a creditor of the deceased person who fails to present a claim to the court or personal representative within a certain period of time after publication of the Notice to Creditors, is out of luck and cannot bring any legal action to collect any bill which the deceased person owed to that creditor.

Unless your state has a law which allows estates settled under living trusts to cut off creditor claims in this manner (some now have such laws), the deceased person's creditors may assert their claims for as long as the local statute of limitations permits.

My problem with the probate lawyers concerning this issue is that most people pay their bills, or their bills are paid when they die, and so there aren't any creditors out there who need to have their claims "cut off." This benefit of probate doesn't do most people any good. If, however, by reason of the deceased person's business or profession there may be unknown or future claimants (such as malpractice claims against a professional), probating that person's estate would be a very good idea, so the heirs won't have to worry about future claims once the time for filing claims in the probate proceeding expires.

But even in cases where probate is desirable, the whole estate doesn't have to pass through probate to get the benefits of probate! Some assets can be intentionally left out of a living trust, and taken through probate under a *pour-over* will (we'll talk about these later). Since only a few assets will pass through probate if that strategy is followed, the probate costs will be minimal and all of the rest of the property can be immediately distributed and dealt with under the living trust, without waiting for the probate proceedings to be finalized.

# CHAPTER 2

# ARRANGING FOR NON-PROBATE TRANSFERS

*QUICK PREVIEW*

---

**MAKING A WILL DOES NOT AVOID PROBATE. IN ORDER TO AVOID PROBATE YOU MUST:**

**(1)  GIVE YOUR PROPERTY AWAY WHILE YOU'RE ALIVE; OR**

**(2)  PUT YOUR PROPERTY INTO A JOINT OWNERSHIP WHERE TITLE WILL PASS TO THE OTHER OWNER AT YOUR DEATH IN A NON-PROBATE TRANSFER; OR**

**(3)  ESTABLISH A LIVING TRUST.**

---

It is no surprise that many people decide that they don't need the "benefits" of probate, and wish to make arrangements for non-probate transfers of their assets.

Let's start out by correcting one popular misunderstanding — making a will does *not* avoid probate. A will is a meaningless piece of paper until it becomes effective by being *admitted to probate* in a probate proceeding. Every state has laws which direct who will administer your estate, and who will receive your property, if you have no will of your own. In effect, your state legislature has written a will for you if you don't prepare one of your own.

The main purposes of having a will are to substitute your choices about who will administer your estate, and who will get your property after your death, in place of the choices which were made for you by the state. If you have a valid will, the probate court will follow your directions in these matters, instead of looking at the law books. So, a will directs and controls your probate proceedings, but does not avoid them.

All customary methods for arranging non-probate transfers can be grouped into three categories:

(1) Give Your Property Away While You're Alive;
(2) Put Your Property into Joint Ownership with Someone Else; and
(3) Establish a Living Trust.

We will discuss each of these approaches in the following chapters.

I haven't included the use of life insurance as one of the three customary methods of arranging a non-probate transfer, but it is also an effective means for transferring wealth to others at your death. If you have handled the wording of your beneficiary choices properly, it can do so without those proceeds having to pass through probate. However, if the beneficiary of your life insurance is a minor child, or is a person who is incapacitated or incompetent at the time of your death, the courts may still become involved, even though there won't be a probate proceeding, since it may become necessary to appoint a guardian or conservator to receive and manage the policy proceeds. The use of a trust to serve as beneficiary of your life insurance can avoid the possibility of *any* court involvement. Also, when life insurance is used to transfer wealth, consideration must be given to the estate tax consequences. We will devote considerable attention to the proper handling of life insurance in later chapters.

# CHAPTER 3

# SHOULD YOU GIVE IT AWAY WHILE YOU'RE ALIVE?

*QUICK PREVIEW*

> **LIFETIME GIFTS ARE FINE IF THE PURPOSE IS TO GIVE THE KIDS SOME FINANCIAL HELP.**
>
> **BUT LIFETIME GIFTS USUALLY ARE NOT A GOOD ESTATE PLANNING DEVICE (EXCEPT FOR ESTATES OF MORE THAN $600,000 SINGLE OR $1,200,000 MARRIED).**
>
> **YOU CAN LOSE YOUR FINANCIAL FREEDOM AND INDEPENDENCE (EVEN WITH A RESERVED LIFE ESTATE); YOU MAY BE UNABLE TO DEAL WITH UNEXPECTED FUTURE DEVELOPMENTS; AND IF THE PROPERTY IS WORTH MORE THAN YOUR TAX BASIS, THE IRS WILL PROBABLY BENEFIT MORE FROM THE GIFTS THAN YOUR CHILDREN.**

If you give away your property and assets during your lifetime, the legal question "Who is the new owner?" won't have to be addressed at the time of your death, since you won't own anything at that time. This is, however, the *least desirable* and *most dangerous* method of avoiding probate.

## Gifting Problem #1 —
## Loss of Financial Independence

If you make your children or relatives the legal owners of all of your assets, what are you going to live on the rest of your life? Do you really want to put yourself in the position of having to ask your son for some money if you want some new clothes, or want to take a trip, or buy a new car? Not only is it humiliating to have to ask for the money, but you take the chance that he might say, "NO!" (and you wouldn't be the first person this happened to). Sometimes, especially with your advancing age, the children begin to think that they know better than you whether you need those new clothes, or that trip, or that new car.

The ravage of time on our bodies causes us to lose a lot of freedom to do what we want. No one should have to also lose his or her financial independence, just to avoid probate.

I know of one elderly couple who learned this lesson the hard way. They owned a large ranch, which they had built up from a homestead through a lifetime of work. They fell into the hands of some "estate planners" who showed them some highly sophisticated ways of avoiding federal estate taxes by incorporating the ranch, making gifts of stock to children, and even making "private annuity" stock sales to the children to diminish what they would own at their death. The estate tax planning was sound, but no one thought about the remaining lifetimes of the couple.

Two sons ended up with over 50% of the stock of the ranch. The ink was barely dry on the paperwork when the sons demanded a stockholder meeting, and with the controlling stock the sons voted in a majority of the corporate directors, who promptly fired Dad as president of the corporation. The income from the profitable ranch, which Dad thought he would have to live on, was suddenly gone, and there was nothing he could do about it! You can't disinherit them if they already have it.

That wasn't enough for these two sons — the corporation owned the ranch home where Mom and Dad lived, and where they had raised these two sons. The new company management (the sons) decided that if that house were to be sold they could put the money to better corporate use (bonuses for themselves). They proceeded to sell the home, and the parents were evicted and had to be physically thrown out into the street by the county sheriff.

Fortunately, most children would not treat their parents this way. This elderly couple didn't think their children would treat them that way — but they did, and it happened because the parents allowed themselves to *lose financial control* through the gifts and other tax strategies.

Some people make gifts with a *reserved life estate*.

In such a gift, the donor retains a "life estate" in the property (the right to use the property for life), while legally transferring to the donee ownership of the "remainder" interest (all rights to the property after death of the holder of the life estate). While this gift approach involves less risk to the donor, it has the same drawbacks of loss of control and financial independence as outright gifts. Once the remainder deed has been executed and delivered, the donor cannot sell or mortgage the property without the consent of the holder of the remainder interest, and if the holder of the remainder interest dies first, that interest will pass to whomever legally inherits his or her estate, whether the life tenant approves of such transfer or not. If the remainder is held by an unfriendly party, constant disputes can arise concerning who should pay for repairs and improvements, and whether the life estate holder is taking proper care of the property.

If the total value of your estate will be less than $600,000 ($1,200,000 for a married couple), you don't have to make gifts to save taxes, and you don't have to make gifts to avoid probate. That being the case, I can't understand why anyone would want to adopt, or would recommend to others, an estate plan strategy which causes a person to lose financial independence during the remainder of his or her lifetime.

## Gifting Problem #2 —
## The Future is Not Predictable

If you part with control over substantial assets, and your future needs dramatically change from what you expected them to be, you may face unnecessary hardship.

Or, you may find that "friendly" gifts suddenly turn out to be very unfriendly because of an unexpected turn of future events. Let me give you an example: If you deed your home to your daughter to avoid probate, with the unwritten understanding that you're going to continue living there, that is what I refer to as a "friendly" gift. You are relying on your trust and confidence in her not to throw you out even though she has legal title. (And, if you did this to reduce federal estate taxes, your plan didn't work — your retained use of the property during your lifetime will cause it to be included in your taxable estate even if the deed worked to avoid probate.)

Parents are supposed to die before their children do, but it doesn't always happen that way. What if, in our example, your daughter later dies in an automobile collision during your lifetime? The title to your home will pass to your daughter's heirs— and unless she has left a will leaving the property back to you at her death, and that will withstands any will contests, the title to your home may now be held by her former husband, your son-in-law.

Now we have even more risk with the "friendly" gift, because your former son-in-law may not continue to be so friendly with you as the years pass, especially after a remarriage. Some evening when he and his new spouse are trying to stretch their money to pay the bills, the thought just might cross someone's mind that he legally owns your house and could legally sell it and take the money it if he wants to. Or, he might die, perhaps from injuries in the same fatal auto collision but after surviving your daughter for a few days or weeks (long enough to legally inherit from her). Then, title to your home may end up with his parents, or his brothers and sisters. They may not be nearly as friendly to you, especially if they always thought their son could have done better than marrying your daughter anyway.

Admittedly the situations I have described are unusual; but unusual things happen every day. If there are ways of avoiding probate without taking such risks, doesn't it make sense to protect yourself?

## Gifting Problem #3 —
## You May Not Be Doing Your Children a Favor

We sometimes get so wrapped up in thinking about estate and inheritance taxes, and probate costs, that we forget to think about income taxes. Lifetime gifts of property which is worth more now than you paid for it may result in severe income tax problems for your children.

To understand this problem, you need to think about *capital gains*. What property is worth, and can be sold for, is its *market value*. Your *tax basis* in property is (with some apology to my accountant friends because of oversimplification) what it cost you, plus money you have spent for capital improvement, less the amount of any depreciation you have taken. If the market value of the property is more than your tax basis, the difference between the two will be a capital gain when you sell the property at its market value. The seller must pay income taxes on his or her capital gains.

When you *give* an asset (real estate, stock, or whatever) to someone, you not only give that person the legal title and ownership of that asset, but you also give them your old tax basis. If that person later sells the property, he or she will have a capital gain measured not by its increase in value after the gift, but instead by its increase in value over your old tax basis. For example, if you hold some farm land now worth $60,000, which cost you $20,000 some twenty years ago when you bought it, there is a potential $40,000 capital gain if the property is sold. That amounts to $10,000 or so of federal and state income taxes, depending upon the state involved.

If property passes to someone at your death, whether in a probate or a non-probate transfer, the tax basis automatically *steps up* to whatever the market value of that property was on the date of your death. In our example, then, if instead of gifting the property to your child, you held on to it and passed it to the child at your death, the child's tax basis would be $60,000. If the property was then sold for $60,000 there would be *no capital gain* because the selling price did not exceed the tax basis. No income taxes would have to be paid. If your estate was under $600,000 in value ($1,200,000 for a married couple with proper tax planning), no federal estate taxes would have to be paid. Uncle Sam would never collect any taxes on that $40,000 of appreciation in value which occurred during your lifetime. The gift cost your child $10,000 in income taxes, probably far more than it would have cost to probate that asset, and much more than it would have cost to establish a living trust. You didn't do your child any favor by making that gift!

# CHAPTER 4

# SHOULD YOU PUT YOUR ASSETS INTO JOINT OWNERSHIP?

*QUICK PREVIEW*

> **USING JOINT OWNERSHIP BETWEEN HUSBAND AND WIFE TO AVOID PROBATE MAY NOT BE A GOOD IDEA:**
>
> (1)      **IF EITHER SPOUSE HAS CHILDREN FROM A PREVIOUS MARRIAGE,**
> (2)      **IF IT IS IMPORTANT TO THE SPOUSES TO KEEP A NEW WIFE OR HUSBAND OF THE SURVIVING SPOUSE FROM GETTING HIS OR HER HANDS ON THE DECEASED SPOUSE'S MONEY AND PROPERTY, OR**
> (3)      **IF THE COMBINED VALUE OF THE COUPLE'S ESTATE IS MORE THAN $600,000.**

As an alternative to the outright gift, many people choose to avoid probate by establishing some form of joint ownership of their property. There are several forms of property ownership where title to property will automatically pass from one co-owner to another co-owner upon his or her death. Such title transfers are non-probate transfers.

Examples of such co-ownership arrangements between husband and wife are *community property* and *tenancy by the entireties* (each of which is available in only certain states). A non-probate title transferring co-ownership arrangement which is recognized in all states is *joint tenancy*, and joint tenant co-owners may be, but do not have to be, husband and wife.

> **LEGAL NOTE: Just naming another person as a co-owner does not automatically create a "joint tenancy," as special wording is required to create this legal relationship. If the ownership records for an asset merely name two persons as the owners (and they aren't husband and wife living in a community property state), without additional legal terminology, the interest of one co-owner will not automatically pass at death to the other co-owner.**

To avoid getting entangled in too many legal words, we will use the expression *joint ownership* in this chapter to describe any legal arrangement in which property is owned by two or more persons, and under applicable local laws the ownership interest of a deceased co-owner will automatically pass to the remaining co-owner or co-owners in a non-probate transfer.

## Joint Ownership Between Husband and Wife

At first glance, joint ownership would appear to be a very good way to avoid probate. A lot of people must think so, because husbands and wives all over the nation hold untold numbers of assets in some form of joint ownership. This is consistent with what I often refer to as the "classic American estate plan," in which each spouse says, "If I go first, I want everything to go to my wife/husband, and when we're both gone, we want it to go to the children."

Surely there can't be anything wrong with any practice which is so widely used that people don't even think about handling things any other way — or can there? Is it possible we are simply setting up husband/wife joint ownerships out of habit? As with so many aspects of our "apples and oranges" discussion, the correct answer depends on the unique circumstances of each family. Anyone who says a husband and wife should *always* use joint ownership to avoid probate, or that a husband and wife should *never* use joint ownership to avoid probate, is wrong. The truth is somewhere in between.

If either spouse has children from a previous marriage, using joint ownership may be a mistake. When the ownership passes to the surviving spouse, the survivor owns that real estate, stock, or whatever (we'll simply use the term *property* from now on, to refer to any kind of asset) on a "no strings attached" basis. The surviving spouse has no legal duty to see that any part of that property ever passes to the deceased spouse's prior marriage children. Stepchildren are not legal heirs of the stepparent, and so the deceased spouse's prior-marriage children have no legal inheritance rights from the surviving spouse.

If the surviving spouse is under any obligation to provide for such stepchildren, it is only a moral obligation. The first few years after the deceased spouse's death, that moral obligation will probably be strong. But after many years, particularly after a new marriage and the formation of new relationships with the children of the new spouse, the original strong feeling of moral duty to some other man or woman's children may grow much weaker, and could disappear entirely.

The only way to be *certain* one's prior-marriage children will be provided for by today's spouse, is to use a trust to hold the deceased spouse's property interest, instead passing that interest outright to the survivor through joint ownership. With a trust, provision can be made for the surviving spouse to have the use and benefit of the deceased spouse's interest in the family property, but legally binding rules can be provided which require that all or a designated portion of the deceased spouse's property interest will pass to the prior marriage children.

> **Author's Note: I really hadn't intended to start our discussion of trusts yet, but this is the first concrete example of the "apples and oranges" problem concerning trusts which we have encountered. I used the expression "a trust." What did that mean to you? I didn't say *a living trust*. Trusts can either be *living* or *testamentary*, and**

there is a world of difference. They are indeed apples and oranges. A living trust is set up and begins to function while you are alive, while a testamentary trust is established through the probate court under the terms of your will. In these discussions, if I say that "a trust" will accomplish a certain objective, that means that either the living trust or the testamentary trust will take care of the problem, but one should use some kind of a trust. We'll talk more about the advantages and disadvantages of living and testamentary trusts in a later chapter.

Even if there are no prior-marriage children, some families are very concerned about protecting the family assets in the event the surviving spouse should remarry. In many states, that new spouse will automatically receive from one-third to one-half of all of the survivor's money and property (which would be all of the original couple's property if it all passed to the survivor through joint ownership), just because they were married to one another. Sometimes, but not always, the new spouse's property rights can be reduced or even eliminated by a properly drawn will executed after the marriage, or under the terms of an ante-nuptial property settlement agreement, if the couple enters into such an agreement. And since this will all happen after your death, there will be no way you can be certain your surviving spouse will make such arrangements even where they are legally permitted.

Again, only by avoiding joint ownership, and using a trust to hold your part of the property after your death, can you be certain that should you be the first to die, your share of the family money and property will not end up in the pockets of your surviving spouse's new wife or husband.

If the combined estate of husband and wife exceeds $600,000 in value (or whatever amount the federal estate tax laws may permit to pass tax-free in the future), it will be a *tax catastrophe* to use joint ownership and pass everything to the surviving spouse. Consider the following example:

Assume that a couple's total assets amount to $900,000, and that each spouse owns a one-half interest in everything (each spouse's personal estate would have a value of $450,000, in this example). Husband could leave his one-half interest to anyone he chooses, on a tax-free basis, since his estate is less than $600,000 in value, and Wife could do the same. But, if Husband dies first and leaves his one-half interest to his spouse, she will then own both halves, and the value of her estate when she dies would be $900,000 (assuming no change in values over the years). She can't leave a $900,000 estate tax-free, since only the first $600,000 will avoid federal estate taxes. Under 1991 laws, there will be a federal estate tax bill of about $114,000 when the wife dies, and that will usually have to be paid in cash within a nine-month period of time.

If that couple had not used joint ownership, but had instead used a properly drawn trust, Husband's one-half interest would pass to the beneficiaries of the trust at his death, and not to his surviving spouse. There would be no taxes on this gift, since the value of his half interest was only $450,000. Wife would not be left wanting — the trust could provide that she could direct how the trust assets would be invested, and it could provide that she would receive all of the income from those investments during her lifetime. It should provide that if she ever has a true need for money, to pay for necessities such as food, clothing, housing, transportation, and medical care, the trust can provide for those needs out of the principal. She can even be given certain limited rights to withdraw principal when she wishes, whether she "needs" that money or not.

For federal estate tax purposes, Wife will not be considered as "owning" the property held in trust. Therefore, at her death the value of her estate will be only $450,000 (again, assuming values have remained unchanged). She can leave that estate to whomever she wishes, free from federal estate taxes.

Whatever remains in the trust when the surviving spouse dies, will be distributed to the final *remainder* beneficiaries, as named in the trust document by the deceased spouse prior to his death. No one has the legal right to change those names, unless the trust document grants someone permission to do so. Since the trust assets actually "passed" by reason of Husband's death, and are simply being "distributed" at Wife's death, Uncle

Sam does not get a second chance to impose estate tax on those assets when the wife dies, even though they may have greatly increased in value while held in trust.

Let's review what using the trust accomplished for this couple: All of the surviving spouse's needs were well provided for. Property valued at $900,000 passed to the children without Uncle Sam getting one dime of the family money. If Wife remarried, her new husband could not legally get one dime of money and property held in the trust. Not bad —IRS loses — new spouse loses — and the family gains!

## Joint Ownership Between Family Members Other Than Husband and Wife

*QUICK PREVIEW*

YOU TAKE SERIOUS RISKS WHICH CAN AFFECT YOUR PERSONAL SECURITY WHEN YOU PUT PROPERTY INTO JOINT OWNERSHIP WITH SOMEONE OTHER THAN YOUR SPOUSE.

ALSO, ASSETS HELD IN JOINT OWNERSHIP WILL NOT BE DISTRIBUTED IN ACCORDANCE WITH THE TERMS OF YOUR WILL.

USE OF THE LIVING TRUST ACCOMPLISHES THE SAME PROBATE- AVOIDING OBJECTIVES AS JOINT OWNERSHIP, BUT DOES SO WITHOUT THE RISKS TO YOUR PERSONAL SECURITY, AND WITHOUT THE BURDENSOME RECORD KEEPING NEEDED TO KEEP TRACK OF VARIOUS JOINT OWNERSHIP ASSETS.

Joint ownership can also avoid probate for co-owners who are not husband and wife. Is it a good idea to set up various assets in joint tenancies with your children in order to avoid probate? By now, you already know the answer to that question: "It depends on the circumstances."

The reason many people use joint ownership with a child or relative, instead of an outright gift, is that they don't *really* want to part with the use and enjoyment of the property before they die, and believe that if their names remain on the ownership records they will be assured of having control. It just doesn't work that way.

All of the comments we made above concerning loss of financial control and independence through gifts apply equally to joint ownerships which you establish with other family members. Especially in the case of real estate, you will no longer be able to sell or mortgage the property without the consent of your co-owner. Your co-owner can legally demand his or her share of the proceeds of any joint-ownership stock or property which is sold. And, you have made a gift of a fractional interest in the property (if you name one person as a joint owner, you have given that person a one-half interest) which may be subject to gift tax, and which may present the same income tax problem of no *stepped-up basis* as to that fractional interest.

While joint ownerships are effective probate-avoiding devices after your death, they can result in a financial disaster while you're alive if things go wrong. Another lawyer asked me to consult with him concerning a client's problem, which illustrates this point: The client was a retired widow, who lived in a quiet and secure older neighborhood of the city. We'll call her "Mom." Mom's home was fully paid for and she had enough savings to look toward a comfortable retirement. She had one daughter, herself unmarried, to whom she wished to leave her entire estate.

Hearing about joint ownership, Mom obtained a deed form, and recorded a deed conveying title to her home to herself and her daughter *as joint tenants with right of survivorship* (the magic legal words to create a joint tenancy). Afterwards, the unmarried daughter fell in love and married — very unwisely. Her new husband was a financial scoundrel, and through various devices incurred many debts for which his wife became legally liable. Lawsuits were filed and judgments were obtained against the husband and wife. Mom was sorry to see this happening to her daughter, but didn't realize she would be involved until it was too late.

One day, the sheriff appeared at Mom's house and nailed up a legal notice, announcing that the property had been levied upon to satisfy a judgment against the daughter, and was scheduled to be sold at public auction on the front steps of the county courthouse on a certain time and day. Mom sought immediate legal advice, and it was necessary to explain to her the legal consequences of the joint ownership she had established.

When she put the property into joint ownership with the daughter, she gave the daughter a one-half interest in the property, and established a legal vehicle for transferring the remaining one-half interest to the daughter at her death in a non-probate transfer. But the daughter owned one-half the minute the deed was recorded! Since the daughter owned a half interest in the property, her creditors had the legal right to seize it to satisfy their judgments.

The court cannot saw a house in half to make a physical division of the daughter's half and therefore had to order that the whole house be sold by the sheriff. Mom got to keep half the proceeds, but as you can imagine, an auction sale on the courthouse steps did not bring in anything close to the real value of the house. Mom was out in the street, without enough money to buy a replacement home. Her hopes for a secure and comfortable retirement in familiar surroundings were down the drain. And all just because she tried to avoid probate the wrong way.

You may not think this could happen to you. You may proudly announce to the world how financially stable your children are, so they just wouldn't have such judgments entered against them. But anyone can have an automobile accident, and if there are deaths or serious injuries in the other car a person may be the subject of a multi-million dollar lawsuit with only a half million or less in liability insurance. If the suit is lost, those claimants become judgment creditors, and they will start taking all of the assets in the name of the judgment debtor.

Many states have laws which apply to joint owner-ship bank accounts, so that if a joint tenant's creditors seize a person's account that person can get the money back if he or she can prove to the court that none of the joint owner's money was ac-tually in the account when it was seized. This is some protection, but you will be in court, your money will be tied up until the court makes its decision, and you will have to spend considerable money on attorney fees.

Many people establish joint tenancies without realizing they are doing so, because of something about human nature which I have decided must be in our genes. At a certain age, it seems that human beings are taken over by some uncontrollable urge which draws them to their banks and stock brokers. When they get to the bank or broker's office, they seem to be irresistibly compelled to start putting one child's name after another on their various ac-counts, certificates of deposit, and securities. Some-times when you question people who do this they're not really sure why they did it. Some say, "So the bills can be paid if I get sick," but when you look further you find that they put the child's name on $50,000 of CD's — a little more money than might be needed to pay the electric bill.

If you read the fine print on the signature card you signed when you put a child's name on an account, CD, or stock you will usually find that you have established a joint tenancy with that person. If you have done this, re-read this chapter to understand the risks you are taking.

Also, with the exception of bank accounts in certain states (and even there certain legal procedures have to be followed), any property in joint ownership passes at your death in a nonprobate transfer to the joint owner, and not according to your will. If you have a will which says that your property is to be divided equally between your two children, but you hold an asset in joint ownership with one of the children, that asset will *not* be legally required to be divided with the other child.

Only those assets which pass through probate are governed by the terms of your will. I have had several clients who understand this, and have turned to the living trust because the record keeping required to keep track of all of the joint ownerships, and to keep them in balance among the children, was becoming too burdensome. If a person has two children, and two $10,000 CD's, each in joint ownership with one of the children, and one of the CD's has to be cashed in to provide money for a new car, the child whose name was on that CD just got disinherited unless some other asset of equal value gets put into joint ownership with that child. People with several children and several accounts, CD's or stocks in joint ownership with them find that the task of trying to keep everything in balance is mind-boggling. If everything is held in a living trust, and the living trust says to divide the trust assets equally among the children, probate is still avoided, but the need for all of that worry and separate record keeping goes away.

# CHAPTER 5

# WHAT IS A LIVING TRUST?

*QUICK PREVIEW*

> A *TRUST* CONSISTS OF A THREE-WAY LEGAL RELATIONSHIP BETWEEN A *GRANTOR*, A *TRUSTEE*, AND ONE OR MORE *BENEFICIARIES*.
>
> YOU CAN WEAR MORE THAN ONE HAT, AND YOU CAN BE THE TRUSTEE OF YOUR OWN TRUST.
>
> TRUSTS CAN BE LIVING (CREATED WHILE YOU ARE ALIVE) OR TESTAMENTARY (CREATED AFTER YOU DIE).
>
> LIVING TRUSTS CAN BE REVOCABLE OR IRREVOCABLE.
>
> YOU CAN USE A CORPORATE TRUSTEE OR A PERSONAL TRUSTEE.
>
> ESTATE TAX PLANNING PROVISIONS CAN BE INCLUDED IN A TRUST, BUT SHOULD BE INCLUDED ONLY IF THEY ARE NEEDED.

The third method for avoiding probate is to use what is popularly called a "living trust" (the popular expression is more convenient than the technical term *revocable personal trustee living trust*, which we really should call such a trust). Before we can appreciate the convenience and benefits of such a trust, we must first understand how it works.

Few people have any experience in working with trusts, and even fewer people understand them. Many think that trusts are for the very wealthy, and wouldn't be appropriate for families of modest means. Others think that trusts are estate tax planning vehicles, and that only those who need estate tax planning (estates over $600,000) need to use them. Your banker may imply that if you are going to have a trust, you should always have the bank as your trustee. Your lawyer may think of a trust as something which is set up through the probate court as a part of probating your estate. Your accountant may advise you that trusts have to file "fiduciary" income tax returns and obtain federal tax identification numbers, and that you will have to spend extra money to have those tax returns prepared if you have a trust.

And, as by now you expect, the truth of those statements depends upon what kind of trust the person is talking about, and the circumstances under which that particular type of trust is being used.

Let's start clearing up the confusion by studying some trust law. Incidentally, you may be interested in knowing that a lawyer doesn't have to study the law of trusts to become a lawyer. It's not a required subject in order to practice law in most states. You will know more about the law of trusts after reading the following pages than many lawyers!

## The Three-Way Legal Relationship

In spite of the many kinds of trusts, and the differences between them, there are certain elements which are present in *every* trust. Every trust involves the creation of a three-way legal relationship, but does not necessarily involve three different people.

The *grantor* (some call this person the *trustor*) is the party who creates the trust, and puts money or property into the trust. The *trustee* of the trust is its business manager. The trustee writes the checks, holds the deeds and securities, makes the investments, and generally does all of the things you would expect a business manager to do. Although the trustee manages the trust assets, they do not belong to the trustee personally. The trustee has a *fiduciary* relationship to all other parties in the trust. A fiduciary owes to others the highest duty of loyalty, honesty, and integrity which is recognized by the law. The *beneficiary* of a trust is the person who is taken care of, and whose needs are provided for, by the trust. Every trust has at least one grantor, one trustee, and one beneficiary.

## Some Ancient History

The law of trusts is ancient. It has its basis in the

"common law" (custom and precedent which has the force of law), rather than in specific laws passed by state legislatures and Congress. You can't find the law of trusts in the United States Code, or in the statute books of your state.

It is said that trust law had its origins in England back in the era of the wars called the Great Crusades. When men went away to those wars, they would sometimes be gone for years at a time. While the men were away fighting the war, the family money and property had to be managed and the needs of the family had to be provided for. In that age, it was simply unheard of to have the man's wife handle the business affairs — it was thought that only a man could take care of such matters.

So, the man going off to war would pick a trusted friend, and would place that friend in charge of the family's financial affairs. He would also provide instructions to that friend concerning how the family was to be provided for while the husband and father was away at war. The courts required that the friend follow those instructions.

This example illustrates the three legal relationships of every trust. The man going off to war, who turned the family money and property over to his friend for management, was what we now call the *grantor.* The trusted friend, who managed the money and property and saw to the needs of the family, was what we now call the *trustee,* and the family whose needs were to be provided for were what we now call the *beneficiaries*. The three-way legal relationship among them is what we now call a *trust*.

A knowledge of the ancient origins of the law of trusts helps us to understand many of the important benefits and features of today's trusts. Because the law of trusts was well settled in the common law before the United States of America even existed, it was carried over into the common law of the colonies, and eventually the new nation (at least in 49 of the states — Louisiana, a former French possession, carried over French trust law). In its basic features, therefore, a person can expect the law of trusts to be the same everywhere. There are few, and usually no, variations in trust law from state to state.

The ancient law did not tell the trustee how to take care of the beneficiaries of the trust, or how to manage the money and property entrusted to the trustee by the grantor. The law simply imposed the fiduciary obligation to carry out the wishes of the grantor, as communicated to the trustee (such communication now is customarily in the form of a written document, called a *trust agreement* or *declaration of trust*). This is a very important point in understanding living trusts, as you will see later in this chapter.

## Types of Trusts

This is probably as good a time as any to begin to

review the differences between those trusts which are apples and those which are oranges. Please don't think of these differing types of trusts as being "good" or "bad," because each serves a useful purpose if used under the right circumstances. Apples are good, and so are oranges. They're just different.

Every trust is either a *LIVING* trust or a *TESTAMEN- TARY* trust, depending upon *when* it is created. If you establish a trust during your lifetime, and "fund" that trust by having it actually own property and begin to function as a trust while you're alive, you have formed a living trust. If, on the other hand, you provide in your will that a trust is to be established after your death (and there will have to be a probate for this to happen), such a trust is referred to as a testamentary trust.

Every living trust is either *REVOCABLE* or *IR- REVOCABLE*. If, once the trust has been established, the grantor has reserved the right to change the provisions of the trust and revoke (cancel and ter- minate) the entire trust, such a trust is called a *revocable trust*. If, once established, the grantor can't change his or her mind and cancel the trust, such a trust is an *irrevocable trust*. In later chapters, we'll discuss the circumstances in which each of these types is appropriate.

No generally recognized legal name has been ap- plied to the following two types of trusts, but the differences are extremely important and you'll never really get to the bottom of the apples and oranges problem if you don't classify a trust as being of one type or the other. If the trustee of a trust is a bank, trust company, stockbroker firm, or other financial institution, we will in this book call that trust a *CORPORATE TRUSTEE TRUST*.

If the trustee of the trust is the grantor, or an individual or individuals selected by the grantor (children, relatives, or friends of the grantor), we will call that trust a *PERSONAL TRUSTEE TRUST*.

Another critical difference between trusts is whether that trust contains estate tax planning provisions. As we will discuss, there are provisions one can add to a trust which will permit most families to completely avoid federal estate taxes, and will greatly reduce the amount of such taxes for all families. However, tax planning provisions complicate the life of the surviving spouse after the death of the first spouse. If a person is going to save a lot of tax money, those complications are worth the effort, but if an estate is not in the tax brackets, a trust with such provisions would complicate life without providing any offsetting benefits. We will call the trusts with those estate tax planning provisions ESTATE TAX PLANNING trusts.

The following list may help you to understand why a person who simply talks about a "trust," without further clarification, can cause great confusion in the mind of someone who doesn't know of these differences. The trust that person is talking about could be any one of the following (and if you get confused reading this list don't be concerned — that's the point of the list!):

**REVOCABLE TRUSTS:**
> LIVING CORPORATE TRUSTEE TRUST
> LIVING CORPORATE TRUSTEE ESTATE TAX PLANNING TRUST
> LIVING PERSONAL TRUSTEE TRUST
> LIVING PERSONAL TRUSTEE ESTATE TAX PLANNING TRUST

**IRREVOCABLE TRUSTS:**
> LIVING CORPORATE TRUSTEE TRUST
> LIVING CORPORATE TRUSTEE ESTATE TAX PLANNING TRUST
> LIVING PERSONAL TRUSTEE TRUST
> LIVING PERSONAL TRUSTEE ESTATE TAX PLANNING TRUST

**TESTAMENTARY TRUSTS:**
> CORPORATE TRUSTEE TRUST
> CORPORATE TRUSTEE ESTATE TAX PLANNING TRUST
> PERSONAL TRUSTEE TRUST
> PERSONAL TRUSTEE ESTATE TAX PLANNING TRUST

The accountant who says, "Your estate is under $600,000, so you don't need a trust," *should have said*, "Your estate is under $600,000, so you don't need an *estate tax planning* trust." The lawyer who says, "Trusts are costly, because of the costs you will incur for trustee fees," *should have said*, "If you use a *corporate trustee*, you will incur trustee fees." The person who says, "You'll have to obtain a federal tax identification number and file fiduciary income tax returns if you use a trust," *should have said*, "Unless you use a *revocable personal trustee trust* where you act as trustee, or one of the trustees, you'll have to obtain that number and file those tax returns."

If we're ever going to keep apples and oranges straight when we talk about trusts, we will have to get specific concerning what kind of trust we're talking about, even if other people keep on being confused.

# CHAPTER 6

# AN OVERVIEW OF THE PROBATE-AVOIDING LIVING TRUST

*QUICK PREVIEW*

> **A LIVING TRUST IS CREATED BY A DOCUMENT, USUALLY CALLED A TRUST AGREEMENT OR DECLARATION OF TRUST.**
>
> **THE SAME PERSON MAY ACT AS GRANTOR, TRUSTEE, AND LIFETIME BENEFICIARY OF A LIVING TRUST. THERE IS NO NECESSITY FOR INVOLVING ANYONE ELSE IN THE GRANTOR'S FINANCIAL AFFAIRS, AND THE GRANTOR REMAINS IN COMPLETE CONTROL DURING THE GRANTOR'S LIFETIME.**
>
> **A LIVING TRUST MUST BE *FUNDED* (BY TRANS-FER OF ALL OF THE GRANTOR'S ASSETS TO THE TRUSTEE) FOR PROBATE AVOIDANCE.**

Over the years the common law developed in such a manner as to permit the three legal relationships of a trust (grantor, trustee, beneficiary) to be created without the need for three different *persons* to become involved. In other words, today one can create a trust (as the *grantor*), designate himself or herself as the *trustee* of that trust (often called a *self-trusteed trust*), and designate the person to be taken care of by the trust as himself or herself (the *beneficiary*).

All the law requires is that *eventually* the beneficiary of the trust will be someone other than the grantor. This requirement is automatically met in the typical probate-avoiding living trust, because the trust will include the grantor's instructions concerning who is to receive the trust assets after the grantor's death. I have spoken in the singular in this paragraph, but it should be understood that husband and wife could act as joint grantors, and act as the co-trustees of the trust, and also be the joint beneficiaries of the trust during their lifetimes.

## Establishing a Personal Trustee Living Trust to Avoid Probate

The personal trustee living trust, usually revocable, is of the greatest interest for estate planning purposes. If the grantor is capable of handling his or her own business affairs, the grantor will usually want to act as his or her own trustee as long as the grantor is capable of doing so, instead of using another person or a corporate trustee.

Let's explore how such a trust could be used for the benefit of a person whose estate value is less than $600,000, so that no estate tax planning provisions are required. In our discussions, we will sometimes use the term *probate-avoiding living trust* to describe a personal trustee living trust which is not being used for estate tax planning purposes.

It all starts with a trust agreement (some call it a declaration of trust). This document officially creates the trust, and contains the grantor's detailed instructions concerning how the trust will be managed, and how the trust estate (whatever property has been included in the trust) will eventually be distributed.

Immediately upon signing the trust agreement, the grantor legally transfers *ALL OF HIS OR HER PROPERTY AND ASSETS* to the trust. This is absolutely necessary for the plan to avoid probate to succeed, and we will get into a more detailed discussion of these property transfers (called *funding the trust*) later.

## How the Living Trust Avoids Probate
*QUICK PREVIEW*

A LIVING TRUST AVOIDS PROBATE BECAUSE IT IS A SEPARATE LEGAL "PERSON" WHICH OWNS THE PROPERTY. SINCE THE "PERSON" WHICH OWNS THE PROPERTY DOES NOT DIE WHEN THE GRANTOR DIES, THERE IS NO NECESSITY FOR PROBATE PROCEEDINGS.

THE SUCCESSOR TRUSTEE AUTOMATICALLY BECOMES THE TRUSTEE UPON THE GRANTOR'S DEATH, WITHOUT THE NECESSITY FOR COURT PROCEEDINGS.

**FOR ESTATES WHICH ARE NOT REQUIRED TO FILE FEDERAL ESTATE TAX RETURNS, THE SUCCESSOR TRUSTEE CAN BEGIN TO CARRY OUT THE GRANTOR'S INSTRUCTIONS CONCERNING DISTRIBUTION OF THE TRUST ASSETS IMMEDIATELY FOLLOWING THE GRANTOR'S DEATH.**

**OFTEN A FAMILY MEMBER CAN SERVE AS SUCCESSOR TRUSTEE, WITHOUT HAVING TO INCUR THE EXPENSE OF USING A CORPORATE TRUSTEE. BEFORE SELECTING A CORPORATE TRUSTEE, CONSIDER THE NEED FOR "HEART" IN ADMINISTERING THE TRUST'S AFFAIRS WHEN YOU ARE GONE.**

It will help to understand how the living trust avoids probate if we discuss a few more legal principles. A trust can be thought of as a legal "person" (sometimes called a *legal entity*). In that regard, it is very similar to a corporation, a common form of business organization. A corporation is owned by stockholders, but it owns property, enters into contracts, and transacts business under its own corporate name, not the individual names of its stockholders. It is recognized in the law as a separate "person" from its stockholders.

Probate is required only when the owner of property dies, and a legal question arises concerning who the new owner of that property will be. But when a living trust has been created, it is a separate legal "person" which cannot die. If grantors have made that trust the legal owner of all of their assets, then the legal "owner" of the property does not die when the grantors who created the trust die. If the property owner does not die, there is no need to go to the probate court! It's just that simple.

If the president of a large corporation should die, no one would expect the law to require that the corporation's assets be probated, and of course there is no such requirement. The president's personal estate might have to be probated, but the corporation's assets aren't probated. The same legal principles apply to the living trust. If any assets remain in the personal name of the grantor, and have not been legally transferred to the trustee, those assets are a part of the grantor's personal estate and will usually have to pass through probate. But all assets legally owned by the trustee will avoid probate. This is why it is so important to fully fund a probate-avoiding living trust.

However, since the grantors were serving as trustees of their living trust, the trust no longer has a trustee when both of the grantors have died. And, just as a corporation would replace its deceased president with a new president (or its senior vice-president would automatically become the president), a trust replaces its deceased trustee or trustees with a new trustee, called a *successor trustee*.

When grantors create a trust, one of the important provisions of the trust agreement is the designation of a successor trustee to manage the trust when neither grantor is any longer able to serve in that capacity. The successor trustee may be a personal trustee, or a corporate trustee, as the grantors wish. Two or more persons (often children of the grantor) may be designated as successor co-trustees. The successor trustee *automatically* becomes the trustee when the former trustee (or all of the former co-trustees) become unable to act in that capacity. No court proceedings of any kind are required.

If a grantor designates his son John as successor trustee, all John will have to do after the death of the grantor is to present to each of the banks, savings and loans, stock brokers, and other places holding assets of the trust, proof of grantor's death (usually a death certificate) and proof that he has become the new trustee (usually by presentation of a signed copy of the trust agreement). Typically, financial institutions will prepare new signature cards, showing the successor trustee's name as the authorized signature on the account, *while he or she waits*. Ten minutes later (not ten days or ten months later), the successor trustee can sign checks and begin carrying out the instructions the grantor provided in the trust agreement.

The illustration used in our example assumed that the grantor designated his son John as the successor trustee. If you discuss the establishment of a living trust with your banker or stock broker, he or she will probably try to talk you into using the bank's or broker's trust department as your successor trustee. It is my opinion that the use of the trust department of a bank or stock broker firm is usually a mistake, at least for estates of moderate size (and if your estate is small, the bank can't make enough money from acting as successor trustee to interest your banker).

The advantages of using a corporate trustee are said to be its stability and permanence (at this writing in 1992, there may be some question about this); its ability to handle all of the paperwork and tax return preparation; and its professional management advice. The disadvantages are the cost of those services (generally an annual fee equal to a percentage of all assets, plus a *transaction fee* for every action taken); the turnover of trust department personnel with many banks (the bank may be permanent, but the trust officer familiar with your family's affairs may not be that permanent); the bank's desire to hold only those investments which are easy to manage (they won't keep that rental house in the trust estate for very long after they take over, because the banker doesn't want to worry about someone's stopped-up kitchen sink); and the lack of what I call "heart."

The heart issue bothers me the most. If the trust agreement tells the banker to pay out whatever the surviving spouse needs to live on, many bankers feel compelled, or are legally compelled, to make the survivor *prove* (with receipts and budgets) what the "needs" are, and to prove that he or she really needs to spend money on a particular expense item. Often, the surviving spouse feels he or she has to beg for money from the banker. If you really want your spouse to have to go through such an exercise, use a corporate trustee (bank or trust company) — but your son or daughter might evaluate those needs with more heart and less paperwork.

Another aspect of heart relates to the education of children. There are a lot of decisions which, it seems to me, are just not appropriate for a banker or stock broker: What sort of allowance does Jane need while she is in the sixth grade? Should Sally have a new dress for the prom? Should Johnny get a new car when he starts college, and if so what kind of car? Should Tommy start college at the inexpensive local community college, or should he apply to a private college with $20,000 per year tuition?

For these reasons, my consistent recommendation to clients has always been to use a corporate trustee only in those circumstances in which no family member has sufficient honesty and plain old common sense to carry out the grantor's wishes. Financial and accounting expertise can be hired — heart can't.

# "Living" with the Probate-Avoiding Living Trust

## QUICK PREVIEW

WHEN THE GRANTOR ACTS AS HIS OR HER OWN TRUSTEE, ACCESS TO THE MONEY AND PROPERTY IN THE TRUST IS JUST AS UN-RESTRICTED AS BEFORE THE ASSETS WERE TRANSFERRED TO THE TRUST. THE GRANTOR CAN SPEND OR INVEST THE MONEY AT ANY TIME, IN ANY AMOUNT, FOR ANY PURPOSE DESIRED BY THE GRANTOR.

A SELF-TRUSTEED REVOCABLE LIVING TRUST IS NOT REQUIRED TO FILE FEDERAL FIDUCIARY INCOME TAX RETURNS AND IS NOT REQUIRED TO OBTAIN A FEDERAL TAX IDENTIFICATION NUMBER. INCOME TAXES ARE HANDLED IN THE SAME MANNER, AND TAX CONSEQUENCES OF TRANSACTIONS ARE THE SAME AS, WHEN THE ASSETS WERE HELD IN THE GRANTOR'S PERSONAL NAME. THERE ARE NO LIFETIME INCOME TAX DISADVANTAGES TO THE GRANTOR.

How will the establishment of such a living trust affect the grantor's lifestyle during the remainder of the grantor's lifetime? **Not at all!!** Many people considering the formation of a living trust worry that their access to their money and property will somehow be restricted, or that they won't be able to do what they want to do, if they have a trust. Let's put those fears to rest.

Remember that this is a personal trustee trust. The grantor is the trustee, and so the grantor will be managing his or her own assets. No one else will be involved in the grantor's affairs, and the grantor won't have to ask anyone else's permission before spending money, or buying or selling any property. If a bank or trust company acts as trustee, someone else will *always* be involved in your financial transactions, even though you may have reserved the right to direct the trustee's investments. And, of course, there are no trustee fees to pay while the grantor acts as his or her own trustee.

To better understand the grantor's complete freedom when using a personal trustee trust, we must think back to our discussion of the development of the law of trusts. The law is not concerned with the manner in which the trust's assets are managed, so long as trustee is managing those assets in accordance with the directions provided by the grantor. Since the grantor is the same person as the trustee, it is obvious that the grantor is most likely going to approve of whatever the trustee wants to do! There are no restrictions on the types of investments the grantor may direct the trustee to make: if the grantor wants the trustee to take a certain amount of money and bet it on number 21 at a Nevada casino, the trustee could legally make that risky "investment" for the trust.

A well-drafted personal trustee living trust will

grant to the trustee broad powers to deal in all types of investments, the power to co-sign the grantor's personal notes when the grantor borrows money, and the power to mortgage or otherwise encumber the trust estate as collateral for the personal loans of the grantor, so the grantor will not find credit harder to get because of having the living trust.

And, since the trust is a revocable and amendable trust, if the trustee (who is also the grantor) ever wants to engage in a transaction which has not been specifically authorized in the trust agreement, the grantor can simply amend the trust agreement and grant that authority to the trustee.

There will be only a few occasions during the grantor's lifetime when he or she will have to think about having the trust, usually simply to assure that the trust's name is shown on paperwork. If real estate is purchased, the deed will have to be made out to the grantor, as trustee of the trust; and the same procedure will be followed for purchases of stock or other assets.

I recommend that even the grantor's checking account be legally owned by the trust, to be certain that probate is avoided for that asset as well as the others. It is only necessary that the bank's records reflect this change — the same checks are used, and signed in the same way, as before the trust was formed. When the grantor goes to the grocery store and buys $50 worth of groceries, he or she is legally acting as trustee, providing for the needs (food) of the beneficiary (grantor), but as a practical matter the grantor will just write a check (on the trust's checking account) to pay for the groceries, the same way as before the trust was established. Where husband and wife are the grantors, and they act as co-trustees of their trust, the trust agreement will ordinarily contain a clause permitting either co-trustee to sign checks on the trust checking accounts (otherwise, the bank will require that both of the co-trustees sign each check).

So long as the grantor (or either grantor, in the case of husband and wife) acts as trustee or co-trustee of such a trust, it will be treated as a *grantor trust* for federal income tax purposes. A grantor trust is not required to obtain a separate federal tax identification number, and is not required to file federal fiduciary income tax returns. (For the more technically minded, these provisions are contained in Section 676 of the Internal Revenue Code, and Treasury Regulation 1.671-4(b) and Treasury Regulation 301.6109-1(a)(2). For federal income tax purposes, the grantor will be treated as if he or she still owned the trust assets individually, and the tax consequences of all financial transactions will almost always be exactly the same as if grantor had personally entered into those transactions. *There are absolutely no significant lifetime income tax disadvantages to having a probate-avoiding living trust*. A real "apples and oranges" problem exists in the income tax area, and people who ought to know better frequently tell grantors of self-trusteed living trusts the wrong tax rules. You will find a complete rundown on the correct grantor trust federal income tax rules at the back of this book.

---

On a day-to-day basis, therefore, little thought will be given to the fact that a self-trusteed revocable living trust exists. But when it is needed, it will be there!

When husband and wife have jointly established a living trust, and the first grantor dies, the trust agreement of a probate-avoiding living trust often provides that the surviving grantor will continue as the sole trustee of the trust. With such provisions, there should be no need for any legal proceedings to be taken by the surviving spouse. A visit to the accountant's office will be necessary for any necessary tax return filings, but no visit to an attorney's office should be necessary. When the surviving grantor dies, the living trust really goes to work.

# Security Provisions —
# The Spendthrift Trust

*QUICK PREVIEW*

**MAKING THE LIVING TRUST A *SPENDTHRIFT TRUST* PROTECTS THE GRANTOR'S SECURITY DURING HIS OR HER LIFETIME, SINCE FINANCIAL OR OTHER PROBLEMS IN THE LIVES OF THE BENEFICIARIES CANNOT AFFECT THE ASSETS OF THE TRUST.**

The law has long permitted the grantor of a trust to include provisions which will assure that a beneficiary cannot get his or her hands on the trust property until the time designated by the grantor for distribution of that property to the beneficiary. The beneficiary's spouse and creditors can also be prohibited from access to the trust property as long as the trust continues in effect. A trust containing such provisions is often called a *spendthrift* trust, because the provisions are usually included to protect a spendthrift beneficiary against his or her own imprudence.

When establishing a living trust, it is wise to include spendthrift trust provisions so that during the grantor's lifetime the trust's assets will be protected against financial or other problems which may arise in the lives of the grantor's children. Putting assets into joint ownership with children or other beneficiaries in order to avoid probate involves numerous financial risks, as we have previously discussed. The use of a living trust, with spendthrift trust provisions included, permits probate avoidance without the grantor having to incur those risks.

Even though the grantor of a spendthrift trust is also a beneficiary during the grantor's lifetime, the spendthrift trust provisions should not be counted on to protect against claims of the grantor's own creditors so long as the trust is revocable. Some jurisdictions take the position that a transfer of assets to a revocable trust can be set aside by the grantor's personal creditors (even though the creditors of a beneficiary who is not also the grantor may be barred by the spendthrift trust provisions). In other jurisdictions the grantor's creditors may not be able to directly seek satisfaction of their claims against the trust's assets, but may be able to obtain an order from the court directing the grantor to revoke the trust, thereby regaining personal ownership of the assets formerly in the trust, at which time the grantor's creditors will be in a position to levy upon those assets. Where asset protection during grantor's lifetime is of primary importance, consideration should be given to the *irrevocable living trust* or even an *offshore living trust*, both of which will be discussed in later chapters.

# Amendments

> **THE GRANTOR CAN EASILY CHANGE THE PROVISIONS OF A REVOCABLE LIVING TRUST AT ANY TIME.**
>
> **MANY CHANGES CAN BE MADE WITHOUT THE NEED FOR AN ATTORNEY.**

A *revocable* trust is also amendable, and in fact amendments are much more common than complete revocations. Unlike a will, where amendments must be made with the same formalities as those required for execution of the will itself, amendments to a living trust can be easily made. All that is required is that the changes desired by the grantor be expressed in writing and signed by the grantor. Such changes could be made on a separate piece of paper, or in the margins of the original trust agreement, or by crossing out provisions of the trust agreement with the grantor's signature in the margin affirming that the grantor crossed out those provisions. There is no requirement for those changes to be witnessed or acknowledged before a notary public. Many amendments concerning relatively minor matters can therefore be made by the grantor personally, without incurring the expense of having an attorney draft the amendments.

# CHAPTER 7

# FEDERAL ESTATE TAX PLANNING

*QUICK PREVIEW*

IF THE COMBINED ASSETS OF HUSBAND AND WIFE HAVE A VALUE IN EXCESS OF $600,000, FEDERAL ESTATE TAX PLANNING IS NEEDED.

IN ORDER TO MINIMIZE FEDERAL ESTATE TAXES, A SHELTER TRUST SHOULD BE UTILIZED TO HOLD ALL OR A PART OF THE ESTATE OF THE FIRST SPOUSE TO DIE. SUCH A TRUST "SHELTERS" THOSE ASSETS FROM FEDERAL ESTATE TAXES WHEN THE SURVIVING SPOUSE DIES.

A SHELTER TRUST CAN BE ESTABLISHED AS A TESTAMENTARY TRUST UNDER THE TERMS OF A WILL, OR IT CAN BE ESTABLISHED AS A PART OF A LIVING TRUST. IF A TESTAMENTARY TRUST IS UTILIZED, PROBATE COSTS WILL BE INCURRED IN ORDER TO ACHIEVE THE ESTATE TAX SAVINGS, BUT IF A LIVING TRUST IS UTILIZED THE ESTATE TAX SAVINGS CAN BE OBTAINED WITHOUT THE PROBATE COSTS.

THE MAXIMUM AMOUNT OF PROPERTY WHICH CAN BE INCLUDED TAX FREE IN THE SHELTER TRUST IS PRESENTLY $600,000. ANY

ADDITIONAL ASSETS OWNED BY THE FIRST SPOUSE TO DIE SHOULD EITHER BE LEFT TO THE SURVIVING SPOUSE (CLAIMING THE MARITAL DEDUCTION) OR PLACED IN A QTIP TRUST (ALSO ELIGIBLE FOR THE MARITAL DEDUCTION), IN ORDER TO DEFER THE DUE DATE OF ANY FEDERAL ESTATE TAXES UNTIL THE DEATH OF THE SECOND SPOUSE.

WHEN THE SURVIVING SPOUSE DIES, HE OR SHE MAY LEAVE THE ASSETS LEFT OUTRIGHT TO THE SURVIVOR TO ANYONE HE OR SHE DESIRES, BUT ASSETS PLACED IN A QTIP TRUST MUST PASS TO THE BENEFICIARIES WHO WERE SELECTED PRIOR TO THE DEATH OF THE FIRST SPOUSE.

WHENEVER A SHELTER TRUST IS USED, CONSIDERATION MUST ALWAYS BE GIVEN TO ITS INCOME TAX CONSEQUENCES.

Under today's laws, most people no longer have to be concerned about federal estate taxes, but they are still around, and the rates are still high, for those who are fortunate enough to have larger estates.

As of the time of this writing, an individual is permitted to pass money or property valued at up to $600,000 completely free from federal estate taxes. The gift tax and the estate tax have been "unified," so that the $600,000 *exemption equivalent* may be taken advantage of either (or partly) to make tax-free gifts during lifetime, or to pass property to heirs tax-free at the time of death. Any portion of the $600,000 exemption equivalent which is not used up through lifetime gifting will be available at the time of a person's death.

Gifts of no more than $10,000 during any one year to any one person do not "count" against the lifetime exemption equivalent, no matter how many such gifts are made. If more than $10,000 is given to one person during a year, the donor of the gift may elect to pay gift tax on the excess, or may elect to deduct the portion of the gift in excess of $10,000 from the $600,000 lifetime exemption equivalent which will be available at the time of the donor's death.

Our discussion about estate tax planning will not attempt to deal with the very sophisticated (and complicated) planning devices which extremely wealthy people may employ. We will concentrate our attention on those estate tax savings which can be attained simply by using some form of trust as a part of the estate plan.

We will be discussing only tax planning strategies which will minimize or avoid federal estate taxes, because residents of all states must deal with those taxes. It should be understood that the various states may also impose state death taxes based upon assets owned by their residents, or assets physically located in their states, and space doesn't permit a discussion all of those state laws and their many variations. With very few exceptions, the adoption of an estate plan which will minimize federal estate taxes will automatically operate to minimize the applicable state death taxes. It is possible, however, to completely avoid federal estate taxes and still be subject to state death taxes, and the reader should seek the advice of a competent tax advisor in order to evaluate the potential state tax liability, and to determine whether the federal estate tax plan can be "fine-tuned" to achieve state death tax savings.

The federal estate tax (which we will abbreviate as *FET*) strategies which achieve the most dramatic results are those which can be adopted by married couples before either spouse dies. The choices of an unmarried person, or a widow or widower, are more limited, but we will discuss those choices as well.

In the following discussion, we will consider estate tax planning strategies for money, property, and investments other than policies of life insurance. Life insurance proceeds are also included in a person's taxable estate for FET purposes, and FET planning for life insurance will be discussed later as a separate topic.

## Estate Tax Planning for Married Couples

The typical estate plan falls into an estate tax "trap," carefully provided for in the tax laws by the seemingly attractive "marital deduction." By far the majority of married couples, when asked about their preferred estate plan, will respond, "If I go first, I want to leave everything to my surviving spouse." Congress invites them to do just that, by providing in the federal estate tax laws an *unlimited* marital deduction — you can leave your spouse $1,000,000 or any amount, free from FET, if you desire to do so.

Were the authors of the tax laws just trying to be "nice guys" by providing that unlimited marital deduction? Not likely. Here is what happens:

Let's assume that a couple has accumulated total assets, other than life insurance, having a value of $800,000, and let's further assume that all of those assets are jointly held so that each spouse has a half interest in the total. Each spouse's half interest has a value of $400,000, and since that is less than the exemption equivalent, each spouse could leave his or her half to anyone free from FET. However, if the first spouse to die leaves all of his or her half interest to the surviving spouse, the surviving spouse then owns the entire $800,000, and when the surviving spouse dies that estate will have a value in excess of $600,000, and Uncle Sam will collect about $75,000 from the family with the survivor dies. This couple lost the chance to take advantage of the exemption equivalent when the first spouse died, because everything was left to the surviving spouse.

Let's take the example of another couple, who are a little more well off. Assume that they own

$1,400,000, all in jointly held property. If the first spouse leaves everything to the surviving spouse (claiming the marital deduction to avoid FET when the first spouse dies), the family will have to come up with over $300,000 to pay FET when the survivor dies.

The most elementary form of estate tax planning is to use a trust (sometimes called a *shelter trust*, since it "shelters" assets from FET when the surviving spouse dies) to hold all or a part of the first spouse's estate, instead of passing it all directly to the surviving spouse. The shelter trust can provide a lot of benefits to the surviving spouse and still keep the trust assets from being included in the surviving spouse's taxable estate for FET purposes. The survivor can receive the income from the shelter trust's investments; the shelter trust can provide for any future needs of the survivor for the necessities of life (food, clothing, shelter, transportation, medical care, etc.) if the survivor ever has insufficient funds of his or her own to pay such expenses; and the survivor can even be given the authority to direct the manner in which the shelter trust's assets will be invested. The survivor can be permitted to withdraw principal from the shelter trust each year, provided the total withdrawals in any one year do not exceed 5% of the value of the trust, or $5,000, whichever is more. For all practical purposes, the surviving spouse will have the same economic benefits as would have resulted if the first spouse's property interest had been left outright to the survivor.

There are some limitations: The survivor could not withdraw the principal out of the shelter trust and give it to a new spouse, for example, but most couples feel that is an advantage, and not a disadvantage. Even with all of these benefits to the surviving spouse, however, the IRS will not consider the shelter trust's assets to be owned by the survivor, and will not include those assets in the survivor's taxable estate for FET purposes.

Here is a comparison of the tax consequences for the first couple ($800,000 total assets) using a shelter trust and not using a shelter trust at the death of the first spouse:

| TAX CONSEQUENCES | | |
|---|---|---|
| **ESTATE UNDER $1,200,000** | | |
| **SIMPLE SHELTER TRUST** | **No Trust** | **Shelter** |
| Total Estate | 800,000 | 800,000 |
| Survivor or Survivor's Trust | 800,000 | 400,000 |
| Shelter Trust | 0 | 400,000 |
| Survivor's Taxable Estate | 800,000 | 400,000 |
| FET AT SURVIVOR'S DEATH | 75,000 | 0 |
| **TAX SAVINGS –** | | |
| **"50-50" SHELTER TRUST** | 75,000 | |

For the wealthier couple ($1,400,000 total assets), the comparison is:

| TAX CONSEQUENCES | | |
|---|---|---|
| ESTATE OVER $1,200,000 SIMPLE SHELTER TRUST | No Trust | Shelter |
| Total Estate | 1,400,000 | 1,400,000 |
| Survivor or Survivor's Trust | 1,400,000 | 700,000 |
| Shelter Trust | 0 | 700,000 |
| Survivor's Taxable Estate | 1,400,000 | 700,000 |
| FET AT DEATH OF FIRST SPOUSE (*) | 0 | 37,000 |
| FET AT DEATH OF SECOND SPOUSE | 317,000 | 37,000 |
| TAX SAVINGS – "50-50" SHELTER TRUST | 243,000 | |

**(*) You will see later that a trust can be used to defer the due date of this tax until after the survivor dies.**

These FET savings result from using a trust to hold the interest of the first spouse to die. Either an apple (living) or an orange (testamentary) trust will accomplish the estate tax planning objectives of the grantors, but one or the other will need to be used. If the testamentary trust is utilized, probate costs will be incurred, and if a living trust is utilized, the FET savings will be achieved without having to pay the probate costs.

## Variations on the Standard Plan

The illustrations used above assume that the entire interest of the first spouse was left to the shelter trust, but it doesn't have to be done exactly that way. Our first couple could, if they had wished to do so, have divided the first spouse's share partly to the surviving spouse, and partly to the shelter trust without losing any FET benefits, as long as the surviving spouse's total taxable estate remained $600,000 or less. The tax consequences of this approach would be as follows:

| TAX CONSEQUENCES | | |
|---|---|---|
| **ESTATE UNDER $1,200,000** | | |
| **FIRST $600,000 TO SURVIVOR** | **No Trust** | **Shelter** |
| Total Estate | 800,000 | 800,000 |
| Survivor or Survivor's Trust | 800,000 | 600,000 |
| Shelter Trust | 0 | 200,000 |
| Survivor's Taxable Estate | 800,000 | 600,000 |
| FET AT SURVIVOR'S DEATH | 75,000 | 0 |
| **TAX SAVINGS –** | | |
| **"50-50" SHELTER TRUST** | 75,000 | |

For couples whose total estate value is less than $1,200,000, a choice is therefore always available concerning what portion of the total estate will be sheltered in the shelter trust, and what portion will be available to the surviving spouse. These factors should be considered in making that choice:

(1)  The survivor's ability to freely use and spend the principal will be restricted, with respect to assets held in the shelter trust.

**(Remember the discussion in the introduction to this book, when the surviving spouse complained about not having free access to the family funds after the first spouse died — they may have put such a large portion of the family assets into a shelter trust that the survivor was left with insufficient funds for personal needs, or the trustee's obligation to use shelter trust income and principal for the benefit of the surviving spouse may have been inadequately spelled out in the trust agreement. Also, estate plans written when the exemption equivalent was lower than it is today may establish shelter trusts for estates of less than $600,000, which are no longer needed since those estates wouldn't pay any FET anyway.)**

(2)  However, in event of remarriage of the surviving spouse, there will be no legal way his or her new spouse can receive any part of the assets in the shelter trust. This is of significant concern to many couples.

(3)  Uncle Sam's only chance to collect FET on the assets placed in the shelter trust was at the time of the first spouse's death. Any appreciation in value of those assets during the lifetime of the surviving spouse will *never* be subjected to FET. For this reason, it is generally tax-wise to fund the shelter trust with as many assets as possible without incurring any FET, as long as sufficient assets left outside the shelter trust for the

survivor to live comfortably.

Additional choices are also available to the couple in our other example (estate value $1,400,000). Since no marital deduction is available for the assets placed in the shelter trust, a strict "50-50" division of assets at the death of the first spouse will result in FET becoming due when the first spouse dies if the total estate is over $1,200,000, since the one-half placed in the shelter trust will be more than the exemption equivalent of $600,000 which will be available in the estate of the first spouse.

It is more or less a fundamental principle of estate tax planning (with a few exceptions) that if it appears some FET will have to be paid, arrangements should be made to delay the date when the tax becomes due until after the death of the surviving spouse. After all, the tax laws might change in the future to raise the exemption equivalent — or the surviving spouse may be able to make enough exempt annual gifts to reduce his or her taxable estate — or at least the surviving spouse will have the use of the tax money without any penalty, since no IRS interest accrues on the tax liability until it becomes "due."

The due date of the FET can be delayed by using a combination of the marital deduction and the shelter trust. The estate plan can provide that the maximum portion of the estate of the first spouse to die which will be placed into the shelter trust is an amount equal to the FET exemption equivalent (technically, the amount which can pass tax-free by use of the *unified credit* against estate and gift taxes, and a shelter trust with such a limitation is sometimes referred to as a *credit shelter trust*). The remaining portion of the deceased spouse's estate is left to the surviving spouse, claiming the marital deduction. The tax consequences of such a plan would be as follows:

| TAX CONSEQUENCES | | |
|---|---|---|
| **ESTATE OVER $1,200,000 CREDIT SHELTER TRUST** | **Shelter Trust** | **Credit Shelter** |
| Total Estate | 1,400,000 | 1,400,000 |
| Survivor or Survivor's Trust | 700,000 | 800,000 |
| Shelter Trust | 700,000 | 600,000 |
| Survivor's Taxable Estate | 700,000 | 800,000 |
| FET AT DEATH OF FIRST SPOUSE (*) | 37,000 | 0 |
| FET AT DEATH OF SECOND SPOUSE | 37,000 | 75,000 |
| **ADDITIONAL FET WHEN CREDIT SHELTER TRUST USED TO DEFER PAYMENT OF FET** | 1,000 | |

The total tax bill when the credit shelter trust was used by this couple to defer the due date of the FET until the death of the surviving spouse was only a little more than if the FET had been paid when the first spouse died, but the surviving spouse had the use of, and income from, $37,000 during his or her lifetime which would not otherwise have been available. In effect, there was a $37,000 "loan" from the IRS during the survivor's lifetime, at a cost of $1,000.

A couple should consider the probable life expectancy of the surviving spouse, and the probable income which could be derived from investing the FET money which didn't have to be paid when the first spouse died, in order to decide whether a pure shelter trust or a credit shelter trust should be utilized.

When the total estate exceeds $1,200,000, the balance of the estate of the deceased spouse, after fully funding the credit shelter trust, does not necessarily have to be left *outright* to the surviving spouse in order to be able to claim the marital deduction and postpone the due date for payment of FET. Whatever portion of the estate is left outright to the surviving spouse can be used by the survivor in an unrestricted manner, and can be passed to anyone selected by the surviving spouse when he or she dies. The Internal Revenue Code authorizes a special type of trust arrangement which can be used to obtain the benefits of the marital deduction, but does not permit the surviving spouse to have unrestricted access to the trust principal, and does not permit the survivor any choice as to the disposition of those assets at the time of his or her death.

This special arrangement is called a *QTIP trust* (Qualified Terminable Interest Property trust). When the deceased spouse's property interest is held in a QTIP trust, the surviving spouse gets all of the income from investment of the QTIP trust assets, and the marital deduction can be claimed for the assets left to the QTIP trust, but the surviving spouse cannot withdraw its principal (however, the trustee can withdraw principal to provide necessities for the surviving spouse when no other funds are available to him or her). When the surviving spouse dies, the assets held in the QTIP trust must be distributed to the beneficiaries which had been selected during the lifetime of the first spouse to die — the survivor cannot change those beneficiaries. If all of this sounds familiar, it should — these are almost the same rules which apply to the shelter trust!

The QTIP arrangement would be helpful when one spouse has children as issue of a prior marriage, and wants to be certain those children are provided for by the survivor, if he or she should be the first to die. The survivor can have the benefit of the assets during the survivor's lifetime, but the assets must absolutely pass to the deceased spouse's children when the surviving spouse dies. Or, it can be helpful if the couple wants to be certain that the survivor does not remarry and divert the assets for the benefit of a new spouse.

The "bad" side of the QTIP trust is that, unlike a shelter trust, the assets of the QTIP trust *will* be included in the taxable estate of the surviving spouse for FET purposes. Unlike the case when the shelter trust is used, appreciation in value of the QTIP trust's assets after the death of the first spouse will not escape FET. For these reasons, many estate planners recommend that the QTIP arrangement should not be used unless the estate is so large that the entire interest of the first spouse to die cannot be placed tax-free in a credit shelter trust.

Let's illustrate the tax consequences for our $1,400,000 estate couple, when a QTIP trust is used:

| TAX CONSEQUENCES | | |
|---|---|---|
| QTIP TRUST COMPARED TO CREDIT SHELTER TRUST | Credit Shelter | QTIP Trust |
| Total Estate | 1,400,000 | 1,400,000 |
| Survivor or Survivor's Trust | 800,000 | 700,000 |
| Shelter Trust | 600,000 | 600,000 |
| QTIP Trust | 0 | 100,000 |
| Survivor's Taxable Estate | 800,000 | 800,000 |
| **FET AT SURVIVOR'S DEATH** | **75,000** | **75,000** |

The QTIP trust is "tax neutral," as compared with the credit shelter trust. There is no additional FET liability, and there are no FET savings. Its only purpose is to restrict the survivor's access to the taxable portion of the deceased spouse's property.

In all of the above discussions, we have referred to leaving assets to the surviving spouse, and the surviving spouse's estate. It should be kept in mind that if a living trust was utilized to accomplish the estate tax planning, the survivor's share will be held in the living trust for probate avoidance when the survivor dies, but those assets will be separately accounted for (often called a *survivor's trust*). The surviving spouse generally serves as trustee of the survivor's trust, and it is usually structured as a revocable trust so the survivor's access to trust principal is unrestricted. Such a survivor's trust continues to qualify as a grantor trust for income tax purposes, so that all of the grantor trust tax benefits are available to the surviving spouse with respect to the property held in the survivor's trust.

## Income Tax Tips and Suggestions

When a shelter trust of any type is utilized, that trust no longer qualifies as a grantor trust since its provisions are irrevocable. It will have to obtain a federal tax identification number and will have to file federal fiduciary income tax returns (although it will generally not have to pay any federal income tax, so long as all of its income is distributed on a current basis).

Persons who prepare living trust documents tend to become casual about income taxes, since there are few tax consequences at the trust level if the trust qualifies as a grantor trust. However, when a shelter trust is utilized, income tax consequences must be given greater attention.

For example, a typical grantor trust easily qualifies as a shareholder of a subchapter S corporation, but a typical shelter trust will not. Special provisions can be included in the trust documents, however, which will permit S corporation stock to be held and accounted for within a special trust which both qualifies as a shelter trust for FET purposes and qualifies as an eligible stockholder of the S corporation. If you have a business organized as an S corporation, be certain that the preparer of your shelter trust documents (whether in a living trust or in your will to establish a testamentary trust) includes those special provisions.

Another matter to consider is the distribution of the income from the shelter trust. Whoever receives its income must pay the income taxes on that income. In our discussions above we have assumed that all of its income will be paid to the surviving spouse; but it doesn't have to be handled that way. If the surviving grantor will have plenty of income to live on, and is in a high income tax bracket, it may be preferable to grant the trustee of the shelter trust the power to "sprinkle" the income among the surviving spouse and the children of the grantors (or even grandchildren) as, in the trustee's discretion, is deemed advisable to provide for each of their individual needs. In many cases, it is better to give the income to a low income tax bracket descendant (to provide for college expenses, for example) than to pay it to a high income tax bracket surviving spouse who will have to hand over a large percentage of that money to the IRS.

# Federal Estate Tax Planning for Unmarried Persons

## QUICK PREVIEW

> **THE MAIN ESTATE TAX PLANNING STRATEGY WHICH IS AVAILABLE TO AN UNMARRIED PERSON IS TO REDUCE THE SIZE OF THAT PERSON'S TAXABLE ESTATE AT THE TIME OF DEATH.**
>
> **LIFETIME GIFTS MAY BE USED TO REDUCE ESTATE SIZE, AND AN IRREVOCABLE TRUST CAN BE ESTABLISHED TO RECEIVE AND MANAGE THOSE GIFTS IF DESIRED BY THE DONOR.**
>
> **A CHARITABLE REMAINDER UNITRUST MAY ALSO BE ESTABLISHED, TO MAKE A CHARITABLE GIFT WHILE RETAINING A LIFETIME INCOME TO THE DONOR. THIS STRATEGY MAY ALSO RESULT IN CERTAIN CURRENT INCOME TAX ADVANTAGES ALONG WITH THE FEDERAL ESTATE TAX SAVINGS.**

There is no opportunity for an unmarried person to reduce the FET bill by using a shelter trust, which greatly limits the tax planning options for such persons. If an unmarried person's estate exceeds the exemption equivalent (presently $600,000) there will be FET to pay when that person dies. Period.

FET planning for unmarried persons must therefore be concentrated upon reducing the amount of their taxable estates. Through use of the annual gift tax exclusion ($10,000 per year per person) on a regular basis, very substantial reductions can be made in the size of the estate. The "price" of that gifting program, of course, is a reduction in assets which are available to the donor during the remainder of his or her lifetime. That price is simply not acceptable to some people, but others who are confident that their remaining assets provide sufficient economic security can achieve significant FET savings through a gifting program.

There are two areas in which a trust can provide helpful assistance in connection with an unmarried person's federal estate tax planning. Sometimes the children or grandchildren to whom gifts could be made to take advantage of the annual gift tax exclusion, are not old enough (or are old enough but not mature enough) to deal responsibly with the gifted money, securities, or property. In those circumstances, it may be wise to establish one or more *irrevocable* trusts for the benefit of those beneficiaries (for example, an education trust to provide for a grandchild's future college education), and to make the annual gifts to those trusts rather than directly to the beneficiaries. If the trust documents are properly drafted, the assets held in such an irrevocable trust will not be included in the donor's taxable estate for FET purposes. A more complete discussion of irrevocable trusts will be found in a later chapter.

A second form of trust can be of great interest to persons (married as well as unmarried) who would like to save on estate taxes by providing some benefits to their church or another charitable organization. The *charitable remainder unitrust* works as follows: The grantor of the trust selects an asset (usually highly appreciated real estate or securities which, if sold, would result in a large income tax bill to the grantor) and gives that asset to the charitable remainder unitrust. The unitrust provides that its assets will be held and invested during the grantor's lifetime, and that the income from those investments (at a rate specified in the trust documents) will be paid to the grantor for life. When the grantor dies, the assets will be turned over to the designated church or charitable organization, and will not be subjected to federal estate taxes in the grantor's estate.

The grantor can act as trustee of the unitrust, and can continue to control the management of the assets during his or her lifetime. Since the trust is a charitable trust, the highly appreciated property or securities contributed by the grantor can be sold by the trust, free from income taxes! The proceeds can then be invested as the trustee (grantor) deems advisable, to provide lifetime income to the grantor.

The grantor will even get an income tax deduction for the year in which the trust was established, but the amount of that deduction will not be the total property value — it is actuarially computed by a rather complex procedure to determine the present value of the future charitable gift when the grantor dies. The shorter the grantor's remaining life expectancy, the higher the current income tax deduction will be; the higher the rate of income the grantor requires be paid back to the grantor from the trust, the lower the current income tax deduction will be, since a high payback will result in smaller amounts accumulating within the trust for the charity.

Some grantors have come up with a clever, and completely legal, way to have the "best of both worlds" when using a charitable remainder unitrust. The grantor takes a part of the income which will be paid back to the grantor from the unitrust, and uses that money to buy a life insurance policy (often in the same face amount as the value of the property given to the unitrust). The life insurance purchase is handled through an irrevocable life insurance trust (discussed in a later chapter), so the policy proceeds won't be subjected to FET when the grantor dies. The end result: The grantor gets a current tax deduction and reduces his or her taxable estate; the church or charity gets a valuable gift; the family gets the same amount of money from the life insurance as they would have if they had inherited the property (actually more, since the inheritance would have been subjected to FET), and *THE IRS GETS NOTHING AT ALL!*

# CHAPTER 8

# THE IRREVOCABLE LIFE INSURANCE TRUST

*QUICK PREVIEW*

LIFE INSURANCE PROCEEDS ARE TAXABLE FOR FEDERAL ESTATE TAX PURPOSES, IF THE INSURED PERSON HOLDS ANY "INCIDENTS OF OWNERSHIP" OVER THE POLICY OF INSURANCE.

IF AN IRREVOCABLE LIFE INSURANCE TRUST (ILIT) IS ESTABLISHED TO OWN THE INSURANCE POLICIES, THE INSURED PERSON NO LONGER OWNS ANY INCIDENTS OF OWNERSHIP, AND THE POLICY PROCEEDS WILL NOT BE SUBJECT TO FEDERAL ESTATE TAXES.

ALL OF THE "GROUND RULES" MUST BE STRICTLY FOLLOWED, ESPECIALLY POWERS OF THE BENEFICIARIES TO WITHDRAW CONTRIBU-TIONS MADE TO THE TRUST INSTEAD OF PERMITTING THE MONEY TO BE USED TO PAY INSURANCE PREMIUMS, IN ORDER FOR THE ILIT TO ACCOMPLISH ITS TAX PLANNING PURPOSES.

ALTHOUGH THE ILIT CANNOT USE THE CASH IT RECEIVES FROM THE INSURANCE TO PAY THE GRANTOR'S TAXES OR DEBTS, IT CAN

> **TRANSFER THAT CASH TO THE GRANTOR'S ESTATE OR LIVING TRUST BY MAKING CASH PURCHASES OF REAL ESTATE OR OTHER ASSETS FROM THE GRANTOR'S ESTATE OR LIVING TRUST.**
>
> **POLICIES WITH CASH VALUES WHICH THE INSURED PERSON MAY WISH TO ACCESS IN THE FUTURE FOR BORROWING OR OTHERWISE, ARE USUALLY NOT PLACED INTO AN ILIT. THE ILIT IS AN IDEAL VEHICLE TO OWN TERM LIFE INSURANCE, OR TO HOLD THE INSURED PERSON'S "INCIDENTS OF OWNERSHIP" OVER GROUP LIFE INSURANCE.**

If there is a policy of life insurance which insures the life of a person, and that person holds any "incidents of ownership" with respect to that life insurance policy, the insurance proceeds paid by the insurance company under that policy must be included in the taxable estate of the deceased insured person for federal estate tax purposes.

You don't have to "own" an insurance policy in the ordinary way, to have an "incident of ownership" over it. The right to designate the beneficiary under the group insurance plan where you work is a sufficient "incident of ownership" to cause the money payable by the insurance company when you die to be included in your estate for FET purposes.

In a community property state, a spouse may be an "owner" of a half interest in the policy because community property money was used to pay the insurance premiums. Therefore, even if the first spouse put the policy in the second spouse's name, as owner, one-half the insurance proceeds may nevertheless be subject to FET if the first spouse used community property funds to pay the premiums.

This presents a "vicious circle" for a person who anticipates that his or her estate is going to have to pay estate taxes, and wishes to maintain a policy of life insurance to provide the funds for payment of those taxes: the policy proceeds will increase the value of the estate and will increase the amount of tax which has to be paid! Extra insurance will have to be carried to provide funds to pay the additional estate taxes on the insurance proceeds, and, of course, that extra insurance will also add to the estate and result in a need for more money to pay estate taxes.

The easy solution to this problem is to establish an *irrevocable life insurance trust* (ILIT) for the purpose of owning the insurance policies. If the ILIT is properly drafted, it will be treated as a separate "person" from the insured party, and if the ILIT holds all of the "incidents of ownership," the insurance proceeds payable when the insured party dies will not be included in the insured person's taxable estate for FET purposes.

All legal rights to designate beneficiaries and make other choices in connection with group life insurance policies can be assigned to the trustee of the ILIT, in order to divest the insured person of all "incidents of ownership."

If money is going to have to be contributed to the ILIT from time to time to provide funds for payment of insurance premiums, a key element in making the ILIT tax plan work is the necessity for inclusion of *Crummey* powers in the trust instrument. (The word *Crummey* isn't intended to be descriptive, even though it is — it was the name of a party involved in the precedent-setting ruling.) These provisions require that if money is contributed to the trust, the beneficiaries of the ILIT may elect to take the money instead of letting it be used to pay the insurance premiums. Because of their legal right to take the money if they want to, the contributed money really becomes "theirs" when it is put into the ILIT. It is therefore the decision of the *beneficiaries*, by not withdrawing the money, to let their money be used to pay the insurance premiums. Because of these provisions, the contributions to the trust are deemed to be "present" gifts to the beneficiaries (but remember the $10,000 annual gift tax exclusion rules, if very expensive policies are involved).

The IRS will look closely at any ILIT arrangement, and the success of the tax plan requires that everything be done strictly "by the book":

1. Someone other than the insured person should be the trustee of the ILIT. In a community property state, I also recommend that the insured person's spouse not be the trustee.

2. The trustee should open a separate checking account for the ILIT. Checks for premium payments should be drawn on that checking account, or automatic withdrawals may be set up from that checking account.

3. The grantor should make cash gifts to the ILIT from time to time to provide funds for premium payments. Preferably funds should not be transferred to the ILIT by a check drawn on a joint account of husband and wife. If such checks must be used, they should *always* be signed by the grantor of the trust, and not by the grantor's spouse.

4. A minimum balance must be maintained in the trust checking account sufficient to remit funds to the beneficiaries if they exercise their right of withdrawal!!! If the grantor transfers funds for the premium payment immediately prior to the payment due date, and the funds are remitted to pay the premium, there will be insufficient funds left in the account to allow the beneficiaries their right of withdrawal unless grantor has *other* funds in the ILIT's account.

5. Written notice must be given to the trust

beneficiaries every time funds are gifted to the ILIT and that notice must advise the beneficiaries of their right to withdraw the funds within a specified number of days following such notification (subject to limitations contained in the trust agreement). If those beneficiaries are minors, give the notice to the parent who is not the grantor of the trust. Develop a standard letter and make photocopies where you simply fill in the date and amount of the gift.

All of this may seem like a lot of bother until you figure out how much FET you are saving by using the ILIT. Your "pay" (in tax savings) for each hour of doing this paperwork is *very* high!

The trustee of an ILIT must not be ordered to make any payment after the death of the grantor which would discharge a legal obligation of the grantor, or of the grantor's estate, because such an instruction will cause the insurance proceeds to be taxable in the grantor's estate. The ILIT's trustee cannot be directed to pay estate taxes due in the grantor's estate, or to pay the grantor's creditors. The ILIT trustee cannot be directed to spend money to educate the grantor's minor children while the grantor is alive, because education of those children is the legal duty of the parent.

One may say, "What is the use of having the ILIT if my family can't use the money to pay these expenses?" The answer is, "Money is money, and it doesn't matter which trust it comes from." The grantor would not have needed the ILIT if the grantor did not own substantial assets (more than $600,000 worth, at a minimum). The critical need is generally to have CASH which can be used to pay the debts and taxes, since it is difficult to pay those bills with real estate, or an interest in a business.

The cash need is satisfied by including an instruction to the trustee of the ILIT to *buy* from the grantor's estate any assets which the personal representative of the estate requests the trustee to buy. So, if the insurance policy paid $200,000 cash to the ILIT after grantor's death, and the grantor (or grantor's living trust) owns a parcel of real estate worth $200,000, the ILIT simply buys that real estate for $200,000 cash. The cash ends up in the grantor's estate (or living trust) and can be used to pay taxes or for any other proper purpose directed in the grantor's will or living trust. The property ends up in the ILIT. Since the ILIT's beneficiaries are usually the same as those under the will or the living trust, the real estate will get to the intended beneficiaries just the same as if it had not been in the ILIT.

In spite of the tax savings which are possible through use of the ILIT, a person may not wish to put *all* of that person's life insurance policies into the ILIT. The insured person will no longer have any rights concerning the insurance policies once they are in the ILIT. Therefore, if your policies have cash values which you may wish to access in the future for borrowing or for other purposes, you may not wish to place those policies into an ILIT. The ILIT is ideal for term life insurance, which has no cash value the grantor might ever want to access, or for use with other policies if the grantor is sufficiently solvent that it is improbable that there would ever be a necessity to access the policy cash values.

# CHAPTER 9

# OTHER IRREVOCABLE LIVING TRUSTS

## Medicaid Eligibility Trust

*QUICK PREVIEW*

> AN IRREVOCABLE TRUST CAN BE USED TO HOLD ASSETS, IN ORDER THAT THOSE ASSETS ARE NOT CONSIDERED AS "AVAILABLE RESOURCES" FOR MEDICAID ELIGIBILITY PURPOSES. THE TRUST AGREEMENT'S PROVISIONS MUST BE CAREFULLY DRAFTED TO MEET MEDICAID TESTS.
>
> A REVOCABLE PROBATE AVOIDING LIVING TRUST CAN BE CONVERTED INTO AN IRREVOCABLE MEDICAID ELIGIBILITY TRUST BY AN AMENDMENT, IF THE GRANTOR EVER DECIDES TO DO SO.

One of the greatest concerns of older Americans is that the need for long term nursing home care will dissipate a lifetime of earnings, and that the nursing home expenses of one spouse may render the other spouse destitute.

There are only two completely satisfactory solutions for these concerns — and one of those is unlikely, and the other is expensive. The unlikely alternative, in the absence of a significant change in the direction of the political "winds" in this country, is that Congress will enact legislation providing meaningful governmental assistance for nursing home patients, without the necessity that the patient first become destitute to qualify for that assistance.

The expensive alternative is long term health care insurance, which will cover nursing home costs. Based upon this author's experience, it is absolutely clear that *if you can afford this insurance, you should obtain it!*\*

While the trust provisions we will discuss below can be helpful under today's laws, there are no guarantees that Medicaid eligibility requirements or benefits will not change in the future, and thereby diminish the benefits from using those trust provisions. After all, if the use of a trust has made you eligible for Medicaid, but Congress eliminates the Medicaid program (unlikely, but possible), meeting the Medicaid eligibility requirements is no longer of much importance.

Medicare doesn't provide much assistance toward payment of long term nursing home costs. Only the Medicaid program provides such help. Medicaid is a joint state and federal program, and although the states cannot change the important federal rules,

---

\*Before purchasing any long term health care insurance policy, try to get a copy of the June, 1991 *Consumer Reports*, and read its excellent article on the subject.

there are variations in the program among the requirements. While it is likely that a plan which meets the federal requirements will also meet local state requirements, I strongly suggest that before adopting any of the following recommendations, the reader should seek advice concerning the state requirements of the state in which he or she resides.

Medicaid eligibility is based upon meeting two main qualification tests: (1) the patient must have substantially exhausted his or her "available resources" (money and property which could be used to pay nursing home bills); and (2) the patient must not have given away resources within the previous 30 months which, had the gift not been made, would have been available for use in payment of the nursing home costs. As is customary with governmental programs, there are many details and qualifications which go with these two tests, but for our purposes we can safely proceed based upon the above general statement of the rules.

When the patient's assets are held in a trust, the assets of the trust are "available resources" of the patient if the patient has the right to take those assets out of the trust, or if the trustee has the discretion to distribute the assets out of the trust to the patient (whether or not such distributions are actually made).

If a person wishes to use a living trust for the dual purpose of probate avoidance and preservation of assets against nursing home costs (which we will sometimes refer to as a *Medicaid eligibility trust*), it is clear that the trust cannot be a revocable trust, since the patient would have the right to take the assets out of the trust by revoking the trust. An irrevocable trust must therefore be used.

And, just *any* irrevocable trust won't do. A Medicaid eligibility trust will generally provide that so long as the grantor is not a nursing home patient, all of the trust *income* will be paid to the grantor (whether income can be protected after the grantor enters the nursing home is not legally certain at this time), but the trust agreement must clearly provide that the grantor (patient) has no right to withdraw *principal*. The trust agreement must also provide that the trustee's discretion to distribute principal to the grantor (patient) is restricted to those amounts which would not disqualify the grantor for benefits under any available program of governmental assistance for which the grantor would otherwise be eligible (since whatever the trustee could distribute will be considered as an "available resource"). The trust agreement should also state that during periods of time when the grantor is an institutionalized nursing home patient, the trustee cannot make any discretionary principal distribution to pay for expense items which would otherwise be provided under an available program of governmental assistance. In order to assure that the trustee's discretion is independently exercised, it is my opinion that the grantor should not be the trustee of a Medicaid eligibility trust.

Merely establishing a Medicaid eligibility trust does not automatically result in the grantor becoming eligible for benefits. Remember that in addition to the available resources eligibility test, there is the second test of not having made a gift of resources within the previous 30 months (actually, there is a formula which determines the period of ineligibility, depending upon the amount of the gift or gifts, but the ineligible period cannot be longer than 30 months). Therefore, regardless of what provisions are included in the trust agreement, the Medicaid eligibility trust must have been in existence long enough to run out the period of ineligibility following the gift to the trust, before there will be any possibility of receiving Medicaid benefits.

It is obvious that such a trust will not be of interest to a healthy person who still wants to handle his or her own financial affairs. But it may be ideal for an elderly person whose health is failing, and who is already turning over the management of many business affairs to the children. One should also keep in mind that a revocable probate-avoiding living trust can always be *amended* in the grantor's later years, to convert it into an irrevocable Medicaid eligibility trust, thereby starting the Medicaid's 30-month ineligibility "clock" ticking before going into a nursing home.

Provisions similar to those included in a Medicaid

eligibility trust can serve as a guideline for the distribution provisions of a regular living trust, if the beneficiary is a disabled person who is currently receiving governmental benefits, in order that the inheritance will not result in a cut-off of those benefits.

When a grantor sets up an irrevocable trust, it does not necessarily mean that the grantor has completely lost control of his or her affairs. Even though the trust can't be totally revoked, the grantor may retain a *power of appointment.* A power of appointment permits the grantor to make changes at any time concerning what persons are to receive the trust estate after the grantor's death. The grantor can also retain the right to approve of all investments made by the trustee, and the right to change trustees if the originally selected trustee is not doing the job properly and is not properly caring for the grantor.

Those retained powers of the grantor are frequently inserted in the trust agreement even though the grantor doesn't intend to exercise them, since the existence of the retained powers will be sufficient to cause the irrevocable trust to be treated as a grantor trust for federal income tax purposes (Section 674 of the Internal Revenue Code). Thus, the grantor's home may be placed into a properly drafted Medicaid eligibility trust for protection, but when that home is sold at a future date during the grantor's lifetime, the tax benefits of the "once in a lifetime, over age 55" exclusion of gain on sale of a personal residence will still be available, as long as the trust remains qualified as a grantor trust.

## ASSET PROTECTION TRUST
*QUICK PREVIEW*

> **A REVOCABLE TRUST PROVIDES LITTLE, IF ANY, PROTECTION AGAINST CLAIMS OF THE GRANTOR'S CREDITORS. IF ASSET PROTECTION IS OF GREAT IMPORTANCE TO THE GRANTOR, CONSIDERATION SHOULD BE GIVEN TO THE ESTABLISHMENT OF AN IRREVOCABLE LIVING TRUST.**
>
> **OFFSHORE LIVING TRUSTS MAY OFFER ADDITIONAL ASSET PROTECTION.**

Some persons are, by reason of occupation or wealth, targets for lawsuits, and have great, and legitimate, concerns about protecting their assets against such claims.

A *revocable* trust provides some protection, but not the total protection such "litigation target" individuals need. About all the revocable trust can accomplish is to slow down the claimants, since they will not only have to sue the grantor and win the lawsuit, but then they will have to go through additional court proceedings in an effort to find some way to reach the trust assets. The law is far from settled in many jurisdictions concerning the extent to which the creditors of the grantor of a revocable trust can reach those assets, and the procedures which must be followed in order to do so. Because of that uncertainty, my uniform advice to clients has always been to consider that a diligent creditor represented by a competent attorney will find a way to reach assets held in a revocable trust.

If asset protection is of primary importance, therefore, consideration must be given to the use of an irrevocable living trust. The grantor will have to weigh the income tax disadvantages, and loss of direct asset control, which accompany the irrevocable living trust, against the benefits to be derived through greater asset protection.

Many litigation target individuals are not only using irrevocable living trusts for asset protection, but they are also establishing those trusts under the laws of offshore countries which will not recognize United States judgments (so long as there was no fraud perpetrated upon the creditor by the grantor of the trust). There are certain nations with stable governments and sound financial systems (such as the Isle of Man) which offer such protection. A detailed discussion of offshore living trusts is outside the scope of this book, but I have used them on several occasions for clients, and it is important to at least mention them here so that those persons who have need for such protection can investigate the possibilities.

# GUIDELINES FOR A SUCCESSFUL ESTATE PLAN

*QUICK PREVIEW*

---

**A SUCCESSFUL ESTATE PLAN SHOULD MEET ALL OF THESE OBJECTIVES:**

(1) PROTECT YOUR SECURITY WHILE YOU'RE ALIVE.

(2) PERMIT YOU TO DEAL WITH FUTURE CHANGES.

(3) PROVIDE FLEXIBILITY SO THAT THE NEEDS OF EACH BENEFICIARY CAN BE PROVIDED FOR ON AN INDIVIDUALIZED BASIS.

(4) PROVIDE PROTECTION AGAINST COURT APPOINTED CONSERVATORS.

(5) AVOID PROBATE WHERE POSSIBLE.

(6) AVOID OR MINIMIZE ESTATE TAXES.

---

In the preceding pages we have discussed many of the techniques which are available for planning the disposition of a person's estate. There are, however, other choices, and new estate planning "vehicles" will undoubtedly be developed in the future. This chapter is intended to provide some general guidelines to emphasize those factors which are most likely to result in a successful estate plan. If you will use these guidelines as a "checklist" of points to consider when evaluating any estate planning proposal, you will seldom if ever make a wrong decision.

## GUIDELINE #1 - PROTECT YOUR SECURITY WHILE YOU'RE ALIVE

The most important person in your estate plan is *you*. Minimizing estate settlement costs helps your family, and is an important consideration in an estate plan. But you don't have to pay those estate settlement costs while you are alive — your family pays them out of your money after you die. If a choice has to be made between saving money for your family, and your personal security while you are still alive, it seems to me that this should be an easy choice — your lifetime security is more important than saving money for your family!

You have already seen that excessive gifting can cause you to lose your financial independence, and can lead to loss of control of your affairs. This is an excellent example of how minimizing settlement costs can threaten your personal security.

Before adopting any estate plan, think carefully about whether it *could* go wrong (no matter how unlikely). Remember that most parents whose children ended up taking advantage of them following an excessive gifting program didn't think their children would do that to them, but they left themselves vulnerable.

I believe that "Murphy's Law" should always be followed in your estate planning — if something *can* go wrong, it will go wrong. Guide yourself accordingly.

## GUIDELINE #2 - BE PREPARED FOR FUTURE CHANGES

Almost the only thing you can count on, when considering the future, is that it probably will turn out to be somewhat different from what you expected. If you adopt an estate planning method which you cannot change in the future, you may regret your actions.

You may not have given consideration to the education of your grandchildren in your estate plan, because your son and his wife are obviously good parents and you are confident they will provide adequately for that education. Relying upon that confidence, you may adopt an estate plan which does not include any provisions for education of grandchildren.

If, however, for reasons you may not understand, the marriage of your son and his wife later breaks up, and the custody of their children is divided (and perhaps one or the other of the parents moves away, or remarries unwisely, or whatever), the good education of your grandchildren may no longer be assured. Or, if your financially secure child is "wiped out" by a business failure, or a liability lawsuit, your child's ability to finance the education of your grandchildren may be destroyed. If you have adopted an estate plan which you cannot change in the future, you will be unable to deal with these new circumstances.

If your clean-cut 14-year-old turns out to be a 24-year-old drug addict, you may regret having made irrevocable provisions to leave part of your estate outright to him or her. If you are unable to change your estate plan to deal with this, you will regret having adopted the plan.

Before making any estate planning move, be absolutely certain that you can change your mind in the future, if you need to. One of the major benefits of a revocable living trust is its ability to be quickly and inexpensively amended.

## GUIDELINE #3 - BE SURE YOUR PLAN IS FLEXIBLE

I use the term "flexible" to refer to the ability to deal with the unique circumstances of each of the beneficiaries of your estate on an individualized basis.

You may have two children, whom you love equally. But if one is a spendthrift with continuous financial problems, and one is prudent, a simple will which says "divide everything equally between my children" would not be wise. Naming the child with financial problems as a co-owner on your certificate of deposit would not be wise. The money and property left to the spendthrift (which you worked so hard to accumulate) will soon be dissipated, doing little good for him or her and no good at all for your grandchildren.

The use of a trust (either a living trust or a testamentary trust) to hold the interest of the spendthrift child is the ideal solution to the problem, because the trust can hold that child's share of your estate, invest it, and provide for the needs of the child in the manner you have directed. If a "spendthrift trust" clause is included in your trust agreement, the child's creditors cannot seize his or her inheritance as long as it is held in the trust, even after your death. And, if you need a trust to accomplish such an objective, I cannot see any good reason to pay probate expenses to get that trust set up through the probate court as a testamentary trust when you could have included the same provisions in a living trust without the probate costs.

The same reasoning, and the same solution, will apply if one of your children has special needs because of a disability. A trust will be required to hold that child's inheritance and provide for the child's needs as you direct.

Chapter 10, *Distribution Plans*, will provide additional suggestions to assure that you achieve maximum flexibility in your estate plan.

## GUIDELINE #4 - PROTECT AGAINST COURT APPOINTED CONSERVATORS

No matter how great your estate plan, if the assets aren't still there at the time of your death the estate plan didn't help anyone very much. The law books are filled with stories of distant relatives, or "black sheep" children, who got themselves appointed by a court as the conservator of an elderly, infirm, or incompetent person and then dissipated the family wealth so that little was left to pass to the heirs when that person died. There are many other stories, not necessarily in the law books, about conservators who refused to provide adequately for the needs of their ward in order to increase the amount of money which would be left for them to inherit when the ward died.

Court-ordered conservatorships sometimes present a "no-win" situation. Some states provide very little supervision over the activities of the conservator, leaving a great opportunity for abuse. However, when close supervision is required there is a constant financial drain on the estate to pay for lawyers and accountants to prepare and file the necessary reports and paperwork with the supervising court.

As you have seen, there are estate planning methods (such as the living trust) which assure that the person or persons of your choice, and not a court-appointed conservator, will administer your financial affairs when you are unable to do so. In addition, the living trust permits you to provide legally binding instructions concerning the manner in which you wish your financial affairs to be handled while you are incapacitated.

## GUIDELINE #5 - AVOID PROBATE WHERE POSSIBLE

If one can safely avoid probate, it is my opinion that it is wise to do so, except in those few instances we have discussed in earlier chapters. However, keep this objective in perspective — it is listed fifth among the guidelines for a very good reason. If you feel that you must make a choice between probate avoidance, and violation of *any* of the first four guidelines listed above, forget about probate avoidance! The other objectives are far more important.

One of the reasons why I consistently recommend the living trust to so many clients is its ability to avoid probate *and also* meet all of the other estate planning objectives and guidelines.

## GUIDELINE #6 - AVOID OR MINIMIZE ESTATE TAXES

If there are two acceptable approaches for accomplishing your estate planning objectives, and *both* meet the first five of these guidelines, it would be wise to select the estate planning vehicle which results in the least possible estate tax liability.

Some of the saddest cases I have encountered in

my law practice have resulted from the actions of people who thought *first* about saving estate taxes and *last* about such matters as their personal security after adoption of the estate plan. Or, more often, those cases have resulted when the advisors, in whom the clients or customers placed their confidence, thought first about estate taxes and last about the personal happiness and security of their clients or customers.

Some estate planning professionals have been known to get "tunnel vision," so that they seem to consider only the tax consequences of an estate planning alternative. Those professionals, although well-meaning, can lead a client or customer into some very unwise choices. Always remember that *you* don't have to pay the estate taxes — they are paid out of your assets after you die, and so you'll never miss the money! No one likes to waste money by paying unnecessary taxes, but if the choice must be made between your lifetime happiness and security, and a higher tax bill after you die, *without exception* make the choice which assures your happiness and security.

The great majority of all estate tax planning methods utilize some form of trust as an essential part of the tax saving plan. If you and your advisors have decided to use a trust for estate tax planning, you should always investigate the possibility of establishing that trust through, or as a part of, a living trust in order to minimize the probate costs and delays.

# CHAPTER 11

# DISTRIBUTION PLANS WHICH SOLVE PROBLEMS

*QUICK PREVIEW*

A LIVING TRUST OFFERS UNLIMITED POS-
SIBILITIES FOR CARRYING OUT THE WISHES
OF THE GRANTOR, EXACTLY AS THE GRANTOR
DESIRES.

A TRULY EFFECTIVE LIVING TRUST IS ONE
WHICH ANTICIPATES FUTURE PROBLEMS, AS
MUCH AS POSSIBLE, AND PROVIDES THE
GRANTOR'S DETAILED DIRECTIONS CONCERN-
ING HOW THOSE PROBLEMS SHOULD BE
HANDLED.

A "BOILER PLATE" LIVING TRUST IS A WASTED
OPPORTUNITY, BECAUSE IT FAILS TO DO SO
MANY THINGS WHICH COULD HAVE BEEN
DONE.

THIS CHAPTER PROVIDES HELPFUL SUGGES-
TIONS FOR PLANS OF DISTRIBUTION AND
FOR DEALING WITH CERTAIN PROBLEMS
WHICH FREQUENTLY ARISE.

Sometimes it is very difficult to decide on the
manner in which the trust estate should be dis-

tributed after the death of the grantor, or grantors. This chapter is intended to provide suggestions for dealing with certain distribution situations which are often encountered.

> **PROBLEM: If one of the grantor's married children should die before the grantor, should any provisions be made for the surviving spouse of the deceased child?**

If the child is married, the grantor must first determine whether any part of the deceased child's share should pass to his or her spouse. Most people adopt a plan of distribution which does not leave anything to the "in-law" side of the family, and instead provide for distribution to the grantor's descendants (grandchildren, great-grandchildren, etc.); however, there are family circumstances in which it is appropriate to provide for the son-in-law or daughter-in-law. When leaving property to the "in-law," however, the grantor must remember that there are no assurances that any part of that property will ever pass to the grantor's descendants. For example, the in-law could remarry and give it all to the new spouse. Some grantors deal with the desire to provide for the in-law by providing that some share of the trust estate will be held in trust during the lifetime of the deceased child's surviving spouse, with certain stated distributions of income or principal required to be made to the surviving spouse during that spouse's lifetime (or until the spouse remarries, if such a provision is desired).

This type of trust provision permits the grantors to provide for the needs of their deceased child's surviving spouse while simultaneously guaranteeing that whatever is not required to be used to care for the surviving spouse must pass to the grantors' grand-children when that surviving spouse dies.

**PROBLEM: If a child of the grantor should die before the grantor, and the grantor does not wish to leave the deceased child's share to his or her surviving spouse, what should be done with that share of the estate?**

Sometimes it is best to deal with this situation on a child-by-child basis: if Mary dies before me, her share should pass to her brother John, but if John dies before me his share should pass to his children, etc.

More often, however, the grantor deals with the circumstance of a deceased child on a family-wide basis, by use of one of two general distribution plans: (1) a *per capita* plan; or (2) a *per stirpes* plan.

In a *per capita* plan of distribution, the grantor provides that whatever remains in the trust estate for distribution to grantor's descendants, will be divided equally among those [...specify relationship, such as children or grandchildren...] who survive the grantor. If a per capita plan is selected, and the grantor has five children, of whom four outlive the grantor, each of the four living children would take one-fourth of the trust estate, and the surviving spouse or descendants of the deceased child would take nothing.

In a *per stirpes* plan of distribution, if a member of the beneficiary group dies before the grantor, the deceased beneficiary's children will take, and share equally among themselves, the inheritance which their deceased parent would have received had he or she lived. If the deceased beneficiary left no children, the property is divided among the grantor's surviving children the same as in the case of a per capita plan. If a per stirpes plan had been directed, in the example used above where one of grantor's five children died before the grantor, and the deceased child left surviving descendants, one-fifth of the trust estate would be distributed to the descendants of the deceased child, and the four living children would each take one-fifth of the trust estate; but if the deceased child left no surviving descendants, the entire trust estate would be divided equally among the grantor's four surviving children. The per stirpes plan of distribution is by far the most often used plan of distribution.

> **PROBLEM: One of grantor's children is simply not able to manage money, so that anything left to that child would soon be lost or wasted.**

A trust provides an ideal arrangement for dealing with this problem. The grantor simply provides that the share of spendthrift child will remain in the trust during that child's lifetime and be managed by the successor trustee.

In the trust agreement the grantor will provide instructions to the trustee concerning how the income and principal of that child's share should be distributed. To avoid misunderstandings and hard feelings between the trustee and the spendthrift child, the grantor should be as specific as possible when giving those instructions. It is generally better to direct that all of the *income* from the share be distributed to the beneficiary, and to provide a schedule (either with reference to a number of payments over a period of years, or for certain amounts to be distributed at certain ages) for principal distributions. It is advisable to include provisions which would permit the trustee to make additional distributions to handle health or other emergency problems, when the trustee determines that help should be given to the beneficiary to handle that emergency.

> **PROBLEM: The grantor has young children at the time the trust is established, and if the grantor should die prematurely those children would not be in a position to manage their inheritance.**

This problem is handled in just about the same way as in the case of the spendthrift child. The trustee can be instructed to hold the beneficiary's share in trust until he or she reaches a specified age. Legal "adulthood" at the age of 18 may not be old enough to assume financial responsibility, and by using a trust the grantor can require that the share be held in trust until any age desired by the grantor, before distribution to the beneficiary. Provision for management of the beneficiary's share by the successor trustee within the trust eliminates the uncertainty and costs which would be involved in having the young person's share managed by some court-appointed "curator" or guardian.

Here again, the more specific the grantor can be in giving distribution instructions to the trustee, the fewer problems the trustee and the beneficiary will have after the grantor's death. For example, the grantor will probably want to provide for distributions to pay education expenses, but the trustee should be given additional guidance: if the beneficiary doesn't need the money (a scholarship or life insurance proceeds, or social security payments, may be available), should the trustee still pay the education expenses? Or, if the beneficiary isn't attending classes and isn't really accomplishing anything, should the trustee keep on paying education expenses? When the grantor directs payment of college expenses, does that include a vocational education program if that is more appropriate for the child?

If the likely beneficiaries are minors and neither parent is living, it is also appropriate to make provision for reimbursement of the child's guardian for expenses incurred in caring for the child.

**PROBLEM: One grantor has "separate proper-
ty" (such as a family inheritance) and wants to
be certain that this property is passed on to
the grantor's children.**

Variation of the same problem: one grantor wants
to be absolutely certain that in the event the surviving spouse should remarry, the new spouse could
not get his or her hands on the deceased spouse's
share of the family property.

Another variation: one grantor has children from
a previous marriage, and wants to be certain that
they will be provided for if he or she dies first.

One way of dealing with these problems is simply
to provide that upon the grantor's death, all
separate property owned by such grantor, or that
grantor's one-half of the family jointly-held property,
is to be left to the children, instead of passing to the
surviving spouse. Sometimes, however, this alternative is not advisable — the surviving spouse may
need the income from all of the property to maintain his or her standard of living, or if the property
in question consists of the house in which the grantors live, the surviving grantor will need to continue
living in that house.

There is a growing trend to deal with these types
of problems by the creation of a *shelter trust* upon
the death of the first spouse, which will hold the
deceased spouse's separate property and/or the
deceased spouse's one-half interest in the family
jointly held property, even though the size of the estate isn't large enough to require creation of such

a shelter trust for estate tax planning purposes. If you will review the shelter trust discussion in Chapter 6, *Federal Estate Tax Planning*, you will see that through use of such a trust the surviving spouse will have the use of the property, and its income, during his or her lifetime, but when the surviving spouse dies the shelter trust's assets *must* be distributed to the beneficiaries designated before the first spouse died.

> **PROBLEM: The grantor wishes to leave certain amounts, or certain assets, to particular beneficiaries, with the balance of the trust estate to be distributed to other beneficiaries.**

Such provisions can easily be inserted into an estate planning document; however, the words used to provide the grantor's directions must be carefully chosen.

It is a legal *rule of construction* (interpretation) of documents that specific gifts are first fully funded before *remainder* gifts. If the grantor expected to have a $200,000 estate, and wanted to leave $100,000 to charity and $100,000 to the grantor's children, there could be two greatly different results depending upon the wording chosen:

If the grantor's trust (or will) said, "Leave $100,000 to the charity, and the remainder of the estate to my children," and it turned out that the value of the estate at the grantor's death was only $150,000, the charity will receive its full $100,000, and the children will receive only the remaining

$50,000. If, on the other hand, the grantor had said, "leave one-half my estate to the charity, and the other one-half to my children," the charity would have received $75,000 and the children would have received $75,000.

Because of these rules of construction, it is often much safer to direct the specific gifts in terms of a percentage or fractional portion of the available estate, instead of using a specific dollar amount.

If a direction is given to leave a certain parcel of real estate, or a particular stock, to a named beneficiary, and at a future date the grantor decides to sell that asset, the gift is said to "fail" — the beneficiary is not entitled to any substitute gift, unless expressly provided for. It is therefore a good idea, when making provisions for distribution of specific items, to clearly state what you want to happen if for any reason that item isn't owned at the time of your death. For example, "Distribute my residence to my daughter Jane," standing alone, will cut off a substantial part of Jane's inheritance if the house is ever sold; but if the grantor had added, "or, if the house is not a part of the trust estate at my death, then distribute $50,000 to Jane," a much more satisfactory result would follow.

Of course, you can always amend your trust or other estate planning document if an asset covered by a specific gift is disposed of, but just in case you forget to do so (or are unable to do so by reason of incapacity) it is certainly wiser to provide specific directions clearly stating your wishes should such a circumstance occur.

> **PROBLEM: The grantor has loaned money to certain children which may not have been repaid at the time of the grantor's death. Or, the grantor has made a lifetime gift to a child, but intends that such gift be deducted from that child's share of the grantor's estate.**

These problems cease to be problems if they are discussed in the estate planning documents. Do you want the loans forgiven? If so, say that. Do you want the unpaid balance of the loan, or the amount of the lifetime gift, deducted from that child's share? If so, say that.

Since all gifts are usually not intended to be deducted from a child's inheritance, and all money advanced to a child is usually not intended to be required to be repaid, misunderstandings among family members after the grantor's death will be minimized by attaching one or more schedules to the grantor's trust agreement, and including provisions in the trust agreement which state that those loans or gifts listed on the attached schedules (as changed and initialed by the grantor from time to time) are intended to be offset from the child's share, but all other loans are forgiven and all gifts not listed on the schedules are not intended to be taken into consideration in the final settlement of the grantor's estate.

The difficult distribution decisions just discussed are not intended to be a complete list of all of the possible problem situations which may arise — they are just the ones that seem to come up the most frequently. The "message" which the reader is intended to receive is that properly prepared estate planning documents should provide, *in detail*, for the unique needs of the grantor's family circumstances. Those documents should, whenever possible, anticipate events which might happen in the future, and state how the grantor would like to have such future events dealt with.

My principal objection to living trust documents prepared by some lawyers who are not experienced in the establishment and operation of trusts, or living trust documents sold by some non-lawyer firms, is the tendency to include "boiler plate" provisions which do not allow for the type of personalized planning which is needed to deal with a particular person's unique circumstances. Sadly, some of them don't even seem to realize that these problems could arise, and they don't even begin to deal with them!

The living trust is a wonderful instrument, which can provide great security to the grantor, and a quick, trouble-free (and argument-free) means for distributing the estate after the grantor's death — if it is used to its full potential. But, like a classic grand piano which can fill an auditorium with great music when played by an expert musician, it can also simply sound like "chopsticks" if its operator doesn't know what he or she is doing.

# CHAPTER 12

# FUNDING YOUR LIVING TRUST

*QUICK PREVIEW*

> **UNLESS YOU LEGALLY TRANSFER ALL OF YOUR MONEY, PROPERTY, AND INVESTMENTS INTO YOUR LIVING TRUST, YOU HAVE PROBABLY WASTED THE MONEY YOU SPENT IN SETTING UP THAT TRUST! PROBATE IS NOT AVOIDED FOR THOSE ASSETS WHICH ARE NOT LEGALLY OWNED IN THE NAME OF THE TRUSTEE OF THE LIVING TRUST.**
>
> **TRANSFERRING ASSETS TAKES SOME TIME, AND SOME MODEST COSTS MAY BE INCURRED, BUT THE RESULTS ARE WELL WORTH THE COST AND EFFORT.**
>
> **THE TIPS AND SUGGESTIONS IN THIS CHAPTER WILL HELP YOU HANDLE YOUR ASSET TRANSFERS WITH A MINIMUM OF PROBLEMS.**

When we speak of "funding" a trust, we mean making the trustee of the trust the legal owner of money, investments, real estate, or other assets. *The most common error made by persons who establish living trusts is their failure to fully fund that trust!* If you do not fully fund your living trust, you have wasted much of the money you spent in establishing that trust. Unless assets are legally owned by the trustee, the benefits of the living trust are not available for those particular assets. Probate is avoided only for the assets owned by the living trust. If there are assets (other than joint ownership assets) which are not legally owned by the trustee, your estate will have to become involved in a probate proceeding to deal with those non-trust assets, even though you have a living trust.

Because of the possibility that some assets may be overlooked, it is common practice to accompany every living trust with a *pour-over will*, which provides that any assets or property which, for any reason, did not get legally transferred to the trustee of the living trust prior to the grantor's death, are left to the trustee of the trust. Those assets will then be added to the trust estate and held, managed, and distributed under the terms of the trust agreement. Such a will assures the grantor that everything will be distributed under the terms of the trust agreement, but probate costs and delays will be incurred in order to probate the pour-over will to get the non-trust assets into the trust. (Such a will also provides the legal vehicle for appointment of guardians of minor children, and if all of the grantor's property is held in a living trust it will not be necessary to probate the will in order for its guardianship provisions to serve their purpose.) Unless you deliberately want to plan your affairs so there will be a probate after your death (sometimes advisable if there may be outstanding or unknown creditor claims which need to be "cut off"), you should transfer legal ownership of *everything* to the trustee. It is sad to see a family have to pay $500 or more in probate costs to handle a small value asset which "just wasn't important enough" to bother with, when the transfer could have been taken care of for the cost of a postage stamp during the grantor's lifetime.

In a self-trustee revocable living trust (the typical probate-avoiding living trust), there are no good reasons for not having the trustee become the legal owner of all of the grantor's assets. As we have previously discussed, the grantor-trustee can deal with those assets just as freely while wearing his or her trustee hat, as if the assets were in the grantor's personal name, and there are no income tax drawbacks to having the assets owned by such a living trust.

I recognize that taking care of the asset transfers is the least enjoyable part of establishing a living trust. But every one of those assets must, someday, be transferred by someone. If you don't take care of the asset transfers during your lifetime, your family will have to do the work when you die, and they will also have to pay probate costs for the privilege of doing that work! Since you know where your records are kept, and where you have accounts and investments, it is always simpler and usually far less expensive for you to take care of the transfers during your lifetime.

Following are some tips and guidelines which may save you time, effort, an d frustration when transferring legal ownership of assets to the trustee of your living trust:

## REAL ESTATE:

A deed must be prepared and placed of record in the office of the county recorder of the county in which the real estate is located. (Some states use different names for this office, but a telephone call to the county courthouse will provide the necessary information.) In most states, your deed should not transfer title to the *trust* itself — instead, it should transfer title to the trustee, "as trustee" of the trust.

**Some states provide homeowner's or other property tax exemptions or discounts for personal residences, and if you live in such a state you should be certain that you contact your assessor or other taxing authority to assure that your exemption or discount is transferred. Also, be certain that your trust agreement clearly provides for your right to use and occupy the real estate for your personal residence, since the exemptions and discounts are usually readily transferable if such provisions are included.**

## RECEIVABLES SECURED BY REAL ESTATE:

If money is owed to you and you hold a promissory note secured by deed of trust or mortgage, or a contract of sale, that receivable must be assigned to the trustee in order that the trustee may collect the money due, and enforce the obligation, in the event of your disability or death.

In the cases of deeds of trust and mortgages, the assignment instruments should be recorded in the office of the county in which the subject property is located. If the deed of trust or mortgage is being collected through an escrow or collection account at a bank or escrow company, a copy of the recorded assignment should be sent or delivered to the escrow or collection agent, and you will usually also need to deposit a new request for reconveyance or satisfaction of mortgage in that account.

## BANK AND SAVINGS ACCOUNTS; CERTIFICATES OF DEPOSIT; SAFE DEPOSIT BOXES:

Bank or savings and loan records and signature cards must be changed to show that the owner of account is the trustee. Usually all that is required is a letter of instructions, signed by all persons who were formerly authorized signers on the account or accounts being transferred. Some, but not all, financial institutions will request a copy of your trust agreement for their confidential records. Usually new accounts and checks are *not* required, with the change being reflected only on the financial institution's records.

If you desire an additional authorized signature on any trust account, be certain that your trust agreement permits you to appoint deputy (assistant) trustees, and then appoint such person as a deputy trustee and have the person entered on the signature card as an authorized signer in that capacity. A deputy trustee does not *own* the money in the trust's account any more than a corporate officer authorized to sign company checks would personally own the company's money in the corporate accounts. Therefore, claims or judgments against the deputy trustee, personally, cannot affect the security of the trust's accounts.

Use the same procedure for transfer of certificates of deposit and safe deposit boxes. Most financial institutions require that you bring in your original certificates of deposit for reissue or endorsement to reflect the new form of ownership. Because of the "grantor trust" nature of the typical living trust, such a transfer is not considered to be an early withdrawal of the certificate of deposit.

In spite of the popularity of the living trust, personnel at some banks and savings and loans are still not fully familiar with the procedures to be followed where accounts are transferred to a self-trusteed revocable living trust. If anyone tells you that your accounts cannot be changed in the manner stated above, or that you must obtain a federal tax identification number for your trust, such person is mistaken! Ask to talk to a manager or supervisor.

## CREDIT UNION ACCOUNTS:

Most credit union accounts will be transferred in the same manner as bank and savings accounts; however, some credit unions may require that your account remain in your personal name, and will not permit transfer to your trust. In such cases, you should designate the trustee as beneficiary of the credit union account in event of your death so the funds will pass to your trust without the need for probate. Your credit union will furnish a form for that purpose.

## SECURITIES (STOCKS, BONDS OTHER THAN U.S. SAVINGS BONDS, MUTUAL FUNDS, MONEY MARKET OR "READY CASH" ACCOUNTS HELD BY STOCK BROKERS):

### MONEY MARKET OR "READY CASH" ACCOUNTS, OR ACCOUNTS WHERE A BROKER FIRM HOLDS YOUR STOCK OR BOND CERTIFICATES

Contact your stock broker, or send a letter of instructions, to request that all securities accounts be transferred to the trustee. Your broker may request a copy of your trust agreement.

### IF YOU HOLD THE STOCK OR BOND CERTIFICATES

All certificates must be delivered to the issuing company or its transfer agent, for transfer to the trustee. A *securities assignment* form is used for this purpose. Your stock broker may be willing to assist you in sending in your certificates for transfer.

A grantor trust *is* qualified to be a stockholder of an S corporation, and such stock may be transferred into the name of the trustee. You should promptly notify your accountant or tax preparer so tax returns will be correctly filed for the S corporation.

### MUTUAL FUNDS

If you hold mutual funds where you deal directly with the fund, a letter of instructions must be sent, advising the fund of your request that the account be transferred to the trustee. Most mutual funds will require that your signature(s) on that letter of instructions be guaranteed by a commercial bank (not a savings and loan or credit union) or a New York Stock Exchange stock broker firm.

### STOCK HELD IN AN EMPLOYEE BENEFIT PLAN

Ownership of unissued securities held in a corporate profit sharing or other benefit plan cannot be transferred until the securities are withdrawn from the plan — see the discussion below concerning company benefit plan beneficiary designations.

## U.S. SAVINGS BONDS:

If you have U.S. Savings Bonds of any series, you may wish to have the ownership changed to the trustee's name. A Treasury Department form is available from your bank which should be completed and sent to the address your bank will provide to you, so that this can be accomplished. The bonds will *not* be considered as having been "cashed in" when transferred in this manner. There are several Treasury Department forms which look similar, and you should make certain that you are using Treasury Form PD 1851, since this is the form which is appropriate for a grantor trust.

## MOBILE HOMES:

Take the original title certificate to your local agency which handles vehicle title transfers. All other documentation is generally provided by that agency while you are there. If title is jointly held by husband and wife, and both grantors do not go to the agency, be certain that the one who presents the documents has a power of attorney to act for the other.

## AUTOMOBILES, BOATS, AIRPLANES, MOTOR HOMES, RECREATION VEHICLES:

Because of possible liability problems, do *not* transfer personal property items of this type to your trust unless you are satisfied that liability insurance is adequate to cover substantial claims, since lawsuits following accidents will almost always involve your trust if title to the vehicle is held by the trustee. Most states have a simple procedure for transfer of vehicle titles in event of death of the owner, and in those states title ownership by the trustee is not necessary to avoid probate costs.

## EQUIPMENT, TOOLS, FARM OR RANCH MACHINERY AND EQUIPMENT, LIVESTOCK, AND OTHER PERSONAL PROPERTY:

Transfers of these types of assets are not filed with any public agency. It is wise, however, to sign a bill of sale confirming the transfer of ownership to the trustee, and to keep that bill of sale with your other important personal records, in order to document the trustee's ownership of the assets.

## LIFE INSURANCE POLICIES NOT INCLUDED IN AN IRREVOCABLE LIFE INSURANCE TRUST:

If you wish the proceeds of your life insurance to be included in the trust estate, and distributed as provided in your trust agreement, the trustee must be shown as primary beneficiary under each policy of life insurance. Change of beneficiary forms should be requested from your insurance agent or from the life insurance policy issuer. Don't forget to change the beneficiary under any group life insurance in connection with your present or previous employment. See the personnel department or other department which administers your employer's benefit programs.

If a policy of life insurance has a cash value, and your living trust includes provisions to protect your assets in event you should require nursing home care, you may wish to consider changing *both* the *ownership* and the *beneficiary* designations for that policy to the trustee's name.

## ANNUITY CONTRACTS:

Tax-deferred annuities should be handled in the same manner as provided below for IRA accounts (beneficiary change only). All other annuity contracts are handled in the same manner as policies of life insurance. For annuity contracts *other than* the tax-deferred annuities, you will probably want to change *both* the *ownership* and the *beneficiary* designations to the trustee's name.

## INDIVIDUAL RETIREMENT (IRA) ACCOUNTS:

Your IRA must remain in your personal name. You may, and should, designate a death beneficiary to receive any unwithdrawn funds from the account (without probate) in event of your death. If married, you will probably want to name your spouse as primary beneficiary, so your IRA balance may be "rolled over" to your spouse's IRA and thereby continue to enjoy the income tax advantages of an IRA account. If the spouse is named as primary beneficiary, the trustee of your trust should be shown as secondary (contingent) beneficiary. If unmarried, you should designate the trustee as primary beneficiary.

## OTHER PERSONAL PENSION
## OR RETIREMENT PLANS

Treatment of Keogh or similar personal pension or retirement plans is the same as in the case of IRA's.

## EMPLOYER-PROVIDED PENSION AND PROFIT SHARING PLANS, AND DEATH BENEFITS:

Great care must be taken to make proper selections under employer provided plans. You should review the plan materials carefully, and discuss the plan with the administrator or your employer's representative having responsibility for the plan, keeping the following general principles in mind:

(1) Your trust will *not* be designated as owner of your vested plan benefits during your lifetime. You must remain the owner until the benefits are withdrawn from the plan.

(2) Your trust should be designated as the death beneficiary to receive any amounts payable under the plan in the event of your death (using the same form of death beneficiary designation as in the case of life insurance), unless you are married and the plan provides survivorship benefits for a spouse. In order to assure that those survivorship benefits will be available to your surviving spouse, he or she should be named as primary beneficiary and the trustee of your trust should be designated as contingent beneficiary to receive any benefits which are payable if you are not survived by your spouse.

Asset transfer is mostly a matter of legwork and letter writing. Most of the work can be done by the grantor(s) of the trust, with little or no cost. The services of an attorney are usually not required, except for preparation of deeds and other real estate transfer papers. Most states treat transfers to a revocable living trust as being exempt from real estate transfer taxes. Transfer agents and stock brokers sometimes charge a fee for handling securities transfers if you hold your own stock and bond certificates, but those fees are usually very modest. It is not customary for any fee to be charged for transfer of brokerage accounts if your broker holds your stock and bond certificates.

If your estate is likely to be in the taxable brackets for federal estate tax purposes (over $600,000 under 1991 law), be certain that you handle insurance and company benefit plan beneficiary designations in the manner recommended by your tax advisor, to assure that you obtain maximum estate tax benefits.

# CHAPTER 13

# TRUST ONLY YOURSELF WITH YOUR TRUST

*QUICK PREVIEW*

> **DON'T BE INTIMIDATED BY LAWYERS OR OTHER ESTATE PLANNING PROFESSIONALS. QUESTION THEIR WORK AND DOUBLE-CHECK IT. MAKE CERTAIN YOUR TRUST AGREEMENT SAYS EXACTLY WHAT YOU WANT IT TO SAY. DON'T COUNT ON THE "GOOD NATURE" OF A SUCCESSOR TRUSTEE TO TAKE CARE OF YOUR ASSETS AND YOUR FAMILY THE WAY YOU WOULD WISH, IF YOU HAVE FAILED TO PRO-VIDE CLEAR AND DETAILED INSTRUCTIONS.**

You are not a lawyer or a professional estate plan-ner, but you had the insight and intelligence to determine that a living trust would be helpful to you and your family. You either retained the services of a recommended attorney to prepare your living trust, or you purchased a commercial living trust product from a reputable company, and you are now the proud owner of a living trust which has been signed and notarized.

The lengthy trust document, and the thick stack of asset transfer documents and other papers, are fair-ly impressive and imposing (and if they aren't, a good job may not have been done for you). Should you just put all of these documents in your safe deposit box or file cabinet and breathe a sigh of relief that this project is now behind you? The answer is, emphatically, **NO!!!**

I have, over the years, interviewed hundreds of clients who brought in their wills, trusts, and other estate plan documents for review and update. More often than not, we found during the course of the document review that there were provisions in the estate plan documents which the clients didn't know were there. In close to half the cases, the estate plan documents contained provisions which the clients did not want, and in many cases there were provisions to which the clients violently objected!

These documents were prepared by apparently qualified attorneys or other estate planning professionals, and in each case the client had relied upon the reputation of the preparer to produce what the client wanted. The client had reviewed the technical legal words without fully understanding them, and had signed the documents more in reliance on the preparer's ability than their own real understanding of what they were signing. The problem, of course, is that although the documents (in most cases, at least) were *legal*, they weren't *right* for the client's circumstances.

The situation I have observed concerning estate planning documents is very similar to the circumstance of a medical patient who, with faith in the "superior knowledge" of the professional, takes a prescription delivered by the pharmacy without first checking to be certain it is the same medicine as the doctor ordered, or who blindly takes the prescribed medication without asking the doctor what that medication treats, what its side effects may be, and why it is appropriate for the patient's problems. The medicine can be perfectly good medicine, but it may not be the *right* medicine for the patient's illness because the patient is taking certain other medication at the same time (and didn't tell the doctor), or due to other unique circumstances of the patient.

Some professionals just don't listen — some listen but decide they will do it their own way because they know they are so brilliant and talented that their decision about what's good for you should be followed whether you like it or not — some just don't take time to explain the documents fully — some are too lazy to change their standard forms to suit your wishes, and others (primarily "do-it-yourself" forms and some non-lawyer "document preparation" companies) just can't change their standard "boiler plate" just for you — and some professionals, being human, just make mistakes.

Don't be intimidated by these experts and professionals! Question what they have done, make them explain the words which have been used, and never let them substitute their judgment for yours when it comes to how your estate is to be distributed and how your family is to be provided for. If you have read this book, you are fully capable of evaluating what they have produced for you, and you have every right to question, and demand explanations for, anything which isn't clear, or which isn't exactly the way you want it.

There are certain parts of estate planning documents in which I most frequently find provisions which were not fully understood by, or approved by, the clients. Pay particular attention to these points:

### Surviving Spouse Provisions

If the surviving spouse is not going to be the trustee of the entire trust after the death of the first spouse, make certain that the words used to describe the trustee's duties toward the surviving spouse say exactly what you want. Lawyers love to use phrases such as this:

> **"Trustee shall distribute to the surviving spouse so much of the principal as Trustee determines to be necessary to provide for the survivor's maintenance, support, and health."**

That seemingly harmless phrase has been the subject of more agony and distress than any other estate plan document phrase of which I am aware, especially if a bank trust department will be involved. Bankers (who seem to hate to part with trust funds, even though they don't belong to the bank) will take these words very literally — if the survivor wants money from the trust to take a vacation trip, he or she can't get it unless the banker can be persuaded the trip is""necessary." A new television set may not be considered as "necessary," or may not be considered as "maintenance" or "support." Money can't be obtained for new clothes unless the banker can be persuaded they are "necessary."

On more than one occasion I have seen trust beneficiaries rendered into beggars before a pompous bank trust officer, trying to get family money released for bona fide family purposes. One shouldn't place the entire blame on the trust officer, however — the attorney who did not draft the trust so as to provide clear instructions bears a good part of the blame. If your trust agreement does not *expressly* describe the circumstances under which you want he surviving spouse to have access to trust funds, get it changed, and do so immediately.

You and your spouse probably worked hard, and jointly, to accumulate your money and property. It is heartbreaking to see a surviving wife or husband find that, in spite of contributing toward building the family wealth, she or he no longer has any voice in what properties and investments are to be sold, or how the proceeds of sale are to be reinvested. If the trust agreement does not *expressly* state that the trustee has to get the surviving spouse's approval for investments, or certain investments, the trustee does not have to get anyone's permission before disposing of the family assets. Just last week, I sat in a room and listened to a trust officer tell a family, where every single family member was in agreement concerning how the funds should be handled, that the bank could care less about the wishes of the widow and family, and would invest the money however it pleased, since the trust agreement didn't give the family any legal right to approve investments.

Unfortunately, the attorney who drafted the trust didn't give the family the right to fire one bank as trustee and move the trust to a different bank. In fact, the creators of the trust were never given the opportunity to decide whether they wanted such a provision included in the trust, and because of their inexperience they didn't even know they could ask for such a provision.

## Provisions Dealing with the Future

Perhaps, for personal reasons, you have decided that the trust funds should be held back and not distributed to your children until they reach a fairly mature age, or should be distributed in installments over a period of years. Many unexpected events may arise during the years those funds are being held in the trust — have you provided any means for "changing the rules" if some future event makes such a change advisable?

Have you allowed the trustee to "invade" principal to provide a life-saving operation for your child or grandchild? The trustee may be legally required to let that person die because the trust agreement doesn't allow the money to be distributed under *any* circumstances for a certain number of years, or until the beneficiaries attain a certain age.

You have provided for availability of funds for your child's education, but have you considered other wise uses of the trust funds which could be advisable? Examples are advancements for a down payment on a home, or to start a business under certain conditions.

Have you directed that the vacation cabin shall not be sold under any circumstances, without allowing some "escape" provision if a gold mine is discovered under the cabin, or the entire family moves 2000 miles away so they can no longer use the property, or some other future development makes it prudent to sell the cabin?

Perhaps the family business which you directed the trustee to operate for 20 years is about to become obsolete because of a technological breakthrough never contemplated during your lifetime. It would be a shame if the trustee had no choice but to operate the business into bankruptcy because the trust agreement failed to contemplate future circumstances which would make sale of the business wise, prudent, and in the best interests of the family.

## Long Term Administration
## by a Non-Family Member

If you have provided for a trust which may continue for years after your death, using a trustee who is not a family member (such as a bank or trust company), have you weighed the *cost* of that long-term administration against the benefits you hope to achieve?

Remember that the revocable living trust which was so simple and inexpensive to administer during your lifetime will turn into a money-eating monster if it continues very long after your death. There will be fees for accountants to prepare fiduciary income tax returns; and there will be trustee's fees and other administrative costs every year for administering the trust. A substantial part of your estate will end up in the pockets of accountants, lawyers, and trustees, and will never reach your family members.

I have found that many estate planning professionals write up long-term trust provisions, as requested by the clients, without ever discussing with those clients the extent of administrative costs the requested long-term provisions would incur. The client may not have wanted the family members to dissipate the estate by reason of their immaturity, but on further consideration the client might just as soon let the beneficiaries have the chance to do something with the money, instead of paying it to non-family members for administrative expenses.

## Per Stirpes and Per Capita

These time-tested legal terms have clear meanings to attorneys and judges, but they certainly are not always clear to their clients. If you find such terms or their equivalents (sometimes the expression *by right of representation* is used instead of *per stirpes*), be certain that you really intend the legal consequences which will follow from the use of those terms.

If your estate is to be distributed to your children per stirpes or by right of representation, and one of your children should die before you, the share of the deceased child will pass in equal shares to the children of the deceased child. Only his or her natural or legally adopted children will participate in the distribution; unadopted stepchildren and surviving spouses will receive nothing. If this is the way you want the distribution handled, no change will be needed in your documents; but if this is not the manner in which you would want a deceased child's share disposed of, you must make changes.

If your estate is to be distributed to your children *per capita*, and one of your children should die before you, *nothing* will pass to the children or surviving spouse of your deceased child, and instead your entire estate will be divided equally among however many of your children are still living at the time of your death. Again, if these are your wishes no change will be necessary, but otherwise you should see that the documents are changed to exactly reflect your desires.

## Irrevocable Trusts Which
## Don't Deliver Results

Many elderly persons establish irrevocable trusts for the purpose of protecting their assets against nursing home costs. If the preparer of the trust was not experienced both in dealing with current Medicaid rules and regulations, and in federal income tax matters, several adverse consequences may arise.

For example, if the trustee is permitted to make discretionary distributions to the grantor who created the trust, the trust is useless for Medicaid eligibility purposes. Medicaid will treat as an "available resource" of the grantor who created the trust *all* trust assets which the trustee could possibly distribute to the grantor (whether the trustee does so or not), and an unrestricted discretionary authority makes it possible for *all* assets to be distributed should the trustee choose to do so. All of the assets in the irrevocable trust would still be "available resources," just as if there were no trust. Many untrained people think that all you have to do to protect your assets is to form an irrevocable trust. This is simply not true.

One should not approach a Medicaid eligibility (irrevocable) trust with "tunnel vision" which looks only toward Medicaid eligibility. In a typical irrevocable trust, many federal income tax benefits are lost, but it is possible to prepare an irrevocable trust which will meed the Medicaid rules without losing personal income tax benefits, by including certain phrases which assure that the trust will be treated as a grantor trust for tax purposes. You'll probably need a good tax person to help you look over your irrevocable trust, but you should make certain that you aren't losing some valuable tax benefits. For example, if the grantor's home is placed in a typical irrevocable trust, and later sold when it appears the grantor will never  be able to return from the nursing home, the $125,000 "once in a lifetime" exclusion of gain from sale of a personal residence will not be available, but if the trust has been drafted so it will be treated as a grantor trust, the income taxes on that $125,000 of gain will be completely avoided.

I have come across several irrevocable trusts in which it is apparent that the preparer gave no thought to the possibility of obtaining valuable income tax benefits while achieving the objective of protecting the assets against nursing home costs.

## Final Disposition —
## Will Probate Still Be Avoided?

As difficult as it may be to believe, I have read fairly decent living trusts, prepared by attorneys, which state that upon the death of the grantor the trustee shall distribute the trust assets to the executor or personal representative of the grantor's estate.

An executor or personal representative is appointed only in connection with probate of an estate. Such a trust provision operates to take all of the assets out of the trust and put them into the probate! What was the point of the living trust, if all of the assets are required to go through probate by being distributed to the estate or its executor or personal representative?

I refer to attorneys who prepare such trusts as "double-dippers," who collect the fee for preparing a living trust while setting it up in such a manner as to assure they still don't lose the chance to collect a second fee for handling probate proceedings (which the living trust could have avoided). I will never know whether such double-dipping was intentional or simply the result of the attorneys' lack of understanding of the true purposes of a living trust. Just make certain your trust agreement doesn't contain such a provision!

# WHAT KIND OF TRUST IS BEST FOR YOU?

If you have completed reading this book, you now know that when someone discusses a "trust," that person not only may be discussing an "apple" or an "orange," but may also be discussing a red apple, or a yellow apple, or a crab apple. All trusts are not the same!

The information you now have should enable you not only to intelligently talk about trusts, but also to become actively involved in deciding whether any kind of trust would be helpful to you and, if so, just what kind of trust provisions are right for your personal, financial, and family needs.

You will also be able to rapidly tell whether the person you are talking to (whether it be a banker, an accountant, an attorney, or a sales representative for living trust products) knows what he or she is talking about!

If you decide you should have a living trust (and I personally believe that almost everyone should have one), it is impossible to advise whether you should purchase a living trust product from a non-lawyer firm, or whether you should have your trust prepared by an attorney. An inexperienced and un-qualified attorney will deliver documents to you which may, frankly, be totally inadequate, while some non-lawyer living trust products on the market are quite superior. On the other hand, there are some non-lawyer living trust products which not only aren't good, but they are downright dangerous! And some skilled attorneys can produce a document package for you which no non-lawyer living trust product can match.

How do you decide what to do? Use your own judgment, based upon the information you now have. Don't buy a living trust product which doesn't permit you to make the kind of detailed choices and decisions you now know you need to make. Don't deal with a sales representative or an attorney who obviously knows less about living trusts than you do.

I am confident that you will now be able to make the right choices.

# INCOME TAX TREATMENT
# OF LIVING TRUSTS

For most purposes, the grantor of a self-trusteed revocable living trust will receive the same income tax consequences with respect to the trust's income and expenses as would have been the case had the trust not been established.

(1) By reason of the revocable nature of the trust agreement, the trust is treated as a *grantor trust* under the provisions of 676 of the Internal Revenue Code. All items of income, deduction, and credit are reported on the grantor's personal income tax return. Treas. Reg. §1.671-4(b).

(2) The trust uses the grantor's personal social security number as its federal tax identification number. Treas. Reg. §301.6109-1(a)(2).

(3) No fiduciary income tax return (Form 1041) is required to be filed so long as the grantor (or one of the grantors, in the case of husband and wife) acts as trustee or co-trustee. Treas. Reg. §301.6109-1(a)(2).

(4) The transfer to the trust is not a "complete" gift, by reason of the reserved power of revocation, and other powers reserved to the grantor. The transfer is therefore not subject to gift tax. Treas. Reg. §25-2511-2(b). Even though no gift tax will be due, the transfer of assets to an irrevocable living trust should be

disclosed on a gift tax return. Treas. Reg. §25-2511-2(j).

(5) Since there has been no "completed" gift, the assets of the trust will be included in the gross estate of the grantor for federal estate tax purposes, and the persons who receive the trust assets upon the grantor's death will receive a "stepped-up basis" for their income tax purposes, the same as if the assets had passed to them in the grantor's estate. Internal Revenue Code §1014(a), §1014(b)(3), and §2038.

(6) As a *grantor trust* the $125,000 "once in a lifetime" exclusion of capital gain upon sale of a personal residence by a person over the age of 55 years will be available even though the trust sells the residence. §121 of the Internal Revenue Code; Revenue Ruling 85-45, 1985-1 C.B. 183.

(7) Capital gain on a residence sale may be "rolled over" if the residence is sold by the trust and the trust purchases another residence for the grantor's use, the same as if the residence sale and purchase had been made by the grantor personally. Revenue Ruling 66-159.

(8) Transfer of installment obligations to a revocable living trust does not "trigger" acceleration and recognition as a "disposition" under IRC §453 or §453B.

Revenue Ruling 74-613.

(9) A *grantor trust* is eligible to be a shareholder of S corporation stock during the grantor's lifetime, and for a limited period after the grantor's death. IRC §1361(c)(2)(A)(i). If your trust agreement includes certain necessary provisions, S corporation stock may also be held in a *shelter trust* after the death of the first grantor.

(10)US Savings Bonds may be transferred to a revocable living trust without triggering gain. Letter Ruling 9009053; Revenue Ruling 64-302.

(11)Gifts from the trust during the grantor's lifetime are considered to have been made by the grantor, and the $10,000 annual exclusion from gift tax will still be available. Treas. Reg. §25-2511-d(f). (In the case of the regular revocable living trust, it is recommended that assets first be withdrawn into the grantor's personal name, and then gifted, rather than being gifted directly from the trust, to assure proper gift tax treatment.)

At the present time there are some differences between the income tax treatment allowed to probate estates for income earned after death, and the income tax treatment of such after-death income when it is earned in a trust. Probate estates receive some income tax advantages which are not available to a trust, but only very large estates are able to receive any real benefits from those provisions of the tax laws. Such differences in tax treatment may soon disappear, however. At this writing two bills were pending in Congress (H.R. 2777 and S. 1394) which would provide that after the grantor's death, a revocable trust will be considered to be an "estate" for federal income tax purposes.

# INSTRUCTIONS FOR
# SUCCESSOR TRUSTEES

The assumption of the office of trustee by the successor trustee of a living trust seldom occurs under pleasant circumstances. The successor trustee ordinarily does not take over management of the trust unless the original trustee (usually a parent) has become seriously ill, or incompetent, or has passed away.

One of the great benefits of a living trust is its ability to handle the transition of control quickly and inexpensively, so that legal matters will not add further troubles to already difficult circumstances.

No court proceedings are required for the successor trustee to assume the office of trustee of a living trust. The succession to office automatically occurs by operation of trust law. The only actions necessary are to inform all banks, stock brokers, or other parties connected with the trust assets and business, that the trusteeship of the trust has changed, and to furnish suitable proof of the identity of the new trustee and his or her authority to act for the trust.

There are only three events which cause the successor trustee to become trustee of the typical living trust: resignation of the original trustee; incapacity or incompetency of the original trustee; or death of the original trustee. It will be necessary for the successor trustee to demonstrate that one of these events has occurred.

Proof of death is simple — just take a copy of the original trustee's death certificate to the bank, broker, or other involved party. Proof of the trustee's resignation is also simple, because the trustee will have signed a letter of resignation. Proof of incapacity or incompetency can be difficult or simple, depending upon whether the trust agreement was properly drafted.

Court proceedings can be held to adjudicate a person as incapacitated or incompetent, but such proceedings can be costly and embarrassing to all concerned. A properly drafted trust agreement can avoid the necessity for such proceedings by providing for an informal determination of incapacity or incompetency, and authorizing all persons dealing with the trust to rely upon that determination. My personal preference is a provision such as the following: "Grantor shall be presumed to be incapacitated or incompetent if all of the following persons who shall themselves then be living and competent, sign a written statement confirming such incapacity or incompetency: Grantor's attending physician, Grantor's spouse, all of Grantor's children [...and add any other names desired by the grantor, such as a brother, sister, minister, or friend...]" If such a provision has been included in the trust agreement, the successor trustee needs only to present a letter signed by that group of people, in order to prove that the original trustee is no longer able to act.

I have found that an afternoon of visits by the successor trustee to banks and others ordinarily takes care of most immediate needs. Take along the trust agreement and the appropriate proof of the occurrence of the event which caused the original trustee to be unable to act. Ordinarily, new signature cards are prepared while you wait, and by the end of the afternoon the successor trustee will be able to write checks, give orders to the stock broker, and take care of all ordinary financial affairs. Of course, letters will have to be sent to out-of-town firms and this will take a few days longer.

One of the most important bits of advice which every successor trustee should follow is to make contact with a qualified accountant right away. You will need to keep a record of all income and expenses, so you can show the other trust beneficiaries that you have honestly handled the money, and a good set of books is invaluable. Follow the accountant's advice concerning preparing a list of assets, which will be accounted for in your trustee records. Proper records eliminate doubt and suspicion, while poor records, which don't provide satisfactory answers, promote discord among family members.

Another reason to see an accountant is that the living trust which was probably exempted from the requirements of obtaining a federal tax identification number, and filing fiduciary income tax returns, while the grantor acted as his or her own trustee, will no longer have that exemption. An accountant can help you obtain the necessary number (often by a telephone call), and all banks and other businesses you deal with will be asking for it.

I also recommend that the successor trustee promptly make a copy of the trust agreement and furnish it to each family member who has a legitimate interest in the estate. You may not be legally required to take such action, but once again I have found that openness eliminates doubts and suspicions, while secrecy promotes discord.

Read the trust agreement carefully to determine what you are directed to do once you become the trustee. You should not need the services of an attorney unless you need assistance in interpreting the instructions contained in the trust agreement.

You don't have to get anyone's permission to take whatever actions the trust agreement tells you to take — so get started right away. If the grantor has passed away, you are free to start distributions right away, as cash becomes available, unless the trust agreement directs you not to distribute assets for a certain number of years, or until some future event occurs. It is not necessary to wait until you are able to distribute the entire trust estate at once. The whole point of the living trust was to permit matters to be handled informally and quickly, with a minimum of legal technicalities. So long as you proceed honestly, you shouldn't have any problems.

# NOTES

# NOTES

# NOTES

# NOTES